FRONTISPIECE.

THE

OLD WORLD

SEEN WITH YOUNG EYES.

New-York:
T. WHITTAKER,
No. 2 Bible House.

1871.

ST. JOHNLAND STEREOTYPE FOUNDRY,
SUFFOLK CO., N. Y.

TO

K. J. D.

THIS RECORD OF MUTUAL EXPERIENCE

IN FOREIGN LANDS

IS AFFECTIONATELY INSCRIBED

BY

HER MOTHER.

PREFACE.

THE following pages were originally written that friends at home might share in the pleasure enjoyed by a party visiting Europe. They were designed, also, to keep the incidents and impressions of that visit alive in the memory of one member of the party, whose young eyes for the first time looked upon the strange scenes, and the wonders of nature and art, which everywhere abound in the old world.

They are simply a jotting down of ordinary events and sight-seeings, and if the "couleur de rose" seems to pervade everything, it is because nothing occurred to mar our pleasure, and it was difficult to prevent that hue from becoming the predominant one.

To those who have been abroad, it is always pleasant to learn the experience of others, and thus recall their own enjoyment; while for those who are anticipating a tour in foreign lands, it is hoped this book may contain some useful suggestions.

C. C. J. D.

THE OLD WORLD

SEEN WITH YOUNG EYES.

STEAMER RUSSIA, *Bay of New York*,
April 22, 18—,

WE are almost "on the wing." So I commence at once to fulfil my promise of keeping a faithful record. The day is bright and warm, and the sea so smooth and calm that it seems to beckon us onward. Our steamer, too, is all we can desire ; and among the ninety-five passengers there are many who will not fail to add to the enjoyment of the voyage. As I sit writing in the saloon, the genial face of Mr. Charles Dickens peeps in, and I am rejoiced to see amongst us that large-hearted man, whose writings have given so much pleasure, and been the solace of many a weary heart.

The saloon is fragrant with the flowers which

have been sent as loving farewells to many on board, and thus a delicious odor of the shore mingles with the fresh air of the sea. One of Mr. Dickens' baskets is very magnificent, being about three feet long, and filled with the most gorgeous flowers, exquisitely arranged. In the centre is the word "Farewell," composed of small white flowers, upon a scarlet ground, while beneath are the initials, "C. D." But the cluster of pure Easter lilies sent to us by our kind friend, Mrs. A., are lovelier and fairer than all, for with these

"The altar's lawn,
At morning's dawn,
We deck at Easter-tide—
To tell of Him
Who liveth, though He died!"

Thursday, April 23.

A pleasant morning and a fair wind. Had a good opportunity to arrange our state-rooms, which are funny little places enough, with their small round port-holes for windows, their narrow shelves for beds, and a rack fastened firmly above the washing slab, containing bottles and tumblers; this firm fastening suggesting the uncomfortable idea of rolling seas, and dismal weather.

The ship is most admirably arranged and appointed, in every respect—the service prompt and efficient—the table bountifully supplied, and everything seems done to secure the safety and comfort of the passengers. At twelve o'clock we had made two hundred and sixty-four miles, having left at half-past three yesterday. The day has been charming in every respect, and most of the passengers were on deck. In the evening we assembled in the saloon, where there was some reading, some talking, some playing of whist, and much drinking of brandy.

Friday, April 24.

"Alack, for me
When I was at sea!"

Said Southey. A remark which I fully appreciated this morning, when the sky was overcast, and the sea so rough that nearly all the passengers kept their state-rooms, and I could hardly lift my head. But the afternoon again found me on deck, enjoying the fresh breeze, and walking up and down the whole length of the ship, which was now plunging from side to side, in a somewhat frantic manner. How glorious it all was, and how I wondered that any one could *help* enjoying it!

I never tired of watching the great green waves, with their snowy tops, rolling so far away, and seeming to break against the sky. I find our state-room, which looked so small at first, has grown pretty large, now that everything is nicely stowed away. It really seems to have "expanded into something quite bulky, and almost boasts a bay-window to view the sea from," as our friend Mr. Boz wrote some years ago. So easy is it to adapt oneself to circumstances.

Sunday, April 26.

This bright, pleasant morning found us crossing the Banks, and the sea was so calm that nearly all the passengers were able to assemble in the cabin for Divine service. Prayers were read by the surgeon of the ship, and all present joined in the service, attentively, if not devoutly. It did not seem a mere form, but a proper recognition of our dependence upon God. Many of the sailors were present, looking very nice in their blue uniforms, and listening with attentive interest. No singing was attempted, it being a hazardous experiment at such a time.

In the afternoon the wind commenced rising, and increased till midnight, by which time it blew a perfect gale. The sea became very rough, and the ship rolled and pitched at a fearful rate. I can enjoy almost anything, I think, but found nothing specially pleasant during this uproarious night. Fortunately, the wind was favorable, and we made good progress.

April 27.

Had a pleasant conversation to-day with Mr. Dickens, who has been suffering much from his lame foot. He says, playfully, that he has "read himself off his legs," but speaks warmly of his "delightful" visit to our own beloved land, and of the great changes and improvements since his former visit. When I congratulated him that he had not encountered one of our terrible railroad accidents, he replied, "I don't pretend to deny that I had some *fears*, for ever since the accident in England where I had so narrow an escape, I have been extremely nervous." It is that terribly destructive accident on the South-eastern railway to which he alludes in "Our Mutual Friend," closing with this paragraph:

"I remember with devout thankfulness that I can never be nearer parting company with my readers forever than I was then, until there shall be written against my life the two words with which I have this day closed this book—THE END."

Mr. Dickens told us that Gadshill, twenty miles from London, where he now resides, was associated with his boyhood, and for that reason he was strongly attached to the spot. That he has won the hearts of the people about him, is evident from the account "Hans Christian Anderson" gives of his charming visit there, and the affectionate regard with which his neighbors of the poorer class spoke of him.

I was much struck with Mr. Dickens' devout manner during the religious services yesterday, and the earnestness of his responses in the beautiful liturgy of the Church of England. Surely, one who has made so many hearts better and brighter, must indeed feel the veneration for the life and lessons of our Saviour, which he does not hesitate to avow.

Friday, May 1.

A beautiful morning, and all on deck watching for the light-houses and cliffs on the Irish coast. Every one seemed very happy in the thought that the voyage was so nearly over, and that beautiful England was close at hand.

My own feelings were, as Artemus Ward used

to say, "very much *mixed.*" The whole voyage had been so thoroughly enjoyable that I had several times exclaimed, "how *can* any one say that it is disagreeable to be at sea? *I* think it *perfectly splendid,* as school-girls say." My few hours of suffering were as nothing compared to my constant pleasure in watching the movements of the ship, the agility of the sailors, and the ocean itself, so wonderful and grand. Then, too, our pleasant fellow-travellers; with whom I had read, and talked, and walked, and with whom I would gladly have been compelled to remain much longer.

Eight days and a few hours, seemed quite too short a passage from New York to Liverpool, and

> "*I*
> Regained my freedom with a sigh;"

being an exception, I fancy, to most voyagers.

Eight o'clock, and a bright moonlit evening, found us at anchor in the Mersey, two miles below our destination; and what a scene of confusion presented itself! Waiters bringing up bags and baskets—ladies arranging cloaks and shawls—gentlemen pointing out their trunks to the Custom-house officers, who had come on board—said officers asking questions, and looking wise, but passing the baggage very rapidly. As fast as an article was passed, and received the label, it was marked for the hotel to which the owner was going. This Babel continued for two mortal hours, but at last we were all on board the passenger tender, and as we steamed away, three rousing cheers were given for the grand old ship, three for the captain, and three for the officers.

When we drove up to the hotel, and the landlady came out with the bright ribbons on her cap, and a face beaming with smiles, a capital specimen of an English landlady, my heart perfectly bounded with delight. When I gave her my Easter lilies, still fresh and beautiful, telling her I had brought her some flowers from America, her face was brighter still. Then the blazing coal fire—the throwing aside of ship clothing—the delightful feeling that the floor beneath you was secure, and would not suddenly become either the ceiling or the side of the room—how pleasant it all was; and I am afraid I almost forgot to be sorry that I had left the beloved ship!

Liverpool, May 4.

The morning after our arrival here found us so fresh and well, that we felt equal to almost anything; so after our letters to the bankers were delivered, we went to the Museum, a fine large structure, with a collection of natural history, statuary, paintings, and an excellent library. The Museum is entirely free — the princely gift of Sir William Brown. We visited the reading-room about twelve o'clock, and found a hundred or more persons seated and reading. What a glorious thing it is to have money, and a disposition with it, to bestow it so nobly!

In the afternoon we had a lovely drive of eighteen miles about the suburbs of Liverpool. The trees are in full leaf, fruit trees in blossom, hedges very luxuriant, and the country looked like a garden. We passed some exquisite residences and grounds; among them, Childwell Abbey, an old country place of the Marquis of Salisbury—a quaint pile of buildings, with some grand old trees on the lawn, in front. The whole drive was enchanting, and we shall not soon forget this first glimpse of "Merrie England."

On our return, there was a muster of the

Liverpool volunteers—many thousands of them—and as they marched past our hotel, we had a very good opportunity of admiring their scarlet uniforms, which looked very brilliant in the light of the setting sun. After they had passed, a performance of Punch and Judy took place under our window, which amused us very much. It is really astonishing how much they can make those puppets do, and how like human beings in miniature they look and act, as they go through their various parts—sometimes fighting, and sometimes having the jolliest time imaginable. A little dog was one of the performers for us, and he looked very oddly, with a broad muslin ruff around his neck, and acted his part with a comic gravity which was perfectly irresistible.

On Sunday we went to St. Bride's Church, with some kind friends. I felt that we were in a foreign land, when I saw the sexton sailing up and down the aisles in a long black gown, something like a clergyman's, only made of some worsted material. There are also some peculiarities in the service. Both creeds are repeated, although at different times. The clergyman gives out the number of the hymn, and the organist immediately commences playing the tune which is to be sung, very simply, during the time the congregation are finding their places. Then the clergyman again gives the number, reads the first two lines, and the singing begins at once. There is also a short prayer—not a *silent* one, after the clergyman goes into the pulpit, and just before he gives out his text.

Sunday afternoon we visited the Blue-Coat Hospital, which interested us very much. We were shown all over it, and admired the exquisite neatness evident everywhere we went. I do not think, however, that the arrangements were very much superior to many of our own charitable institutions, except the bathing facilities, which were admirable. They have a large tank in which the children can be taught to swim, and the water can be let on to the depth of four or five feet, and drawn off at pleasure. The institution accommodates and supports two hundred and fifty boys and one hundred girls, all of whom are dressed in the costume of the establishment, and look oddly enough.

The boys leave at fourteen years of age, and the girls at sixteen. The former wear an entire suit of very dark blue cloth, with a long tailed coat rounded in front like a quaker's. On their necks they wear a white cravat, without any collar, and clergymen's bands. It makes them look like a collection of Lilliputian clergymen; and the garb itself has a tendency to give a serious expression to their faces, which one does not often see in young boys. The girls wear dark blue gowns which reach their ankles, and round white capes made of thick muslin. They all marched into the chapel, to the solemn music of the organ, and took their places very systematically. The exercises were conducted by the children themselves, and consisted of singing, prayers, catechism, and recitation of portions of Scripture. The prayers were read—the hymns given out, and the questions of the catechism asked by boys selected for the purpose; and it was really astonishing to hear their long answers without a single mistake. A great many noble men and women have been educated at this institution, who, but for its sheltering care, would have had no one to teach them the right way.

In the evening we went to St. Mary's Church for the Blind, where they had a full choral service; the blind being the singers. They sang beautifully, and it was very touching to hear their sweet voices, so full of thanksgiving, and remember that those sightless eyes had never seen the exquisite works of their Heavenly Father's hand.

We feel that we have made *much* of Liverpool, which is not generally considered very interesting.

London.

Our journey here by way of the North-western railway was thoroughly pleasant, and the country beautiful in the extreme. The fruit trees were one mass of blossoms, and white cowslips, violets and other flowers covered the meadows. Every foot of ground seemed cultivated, while the hawthorn hedges which everywhere line the road, and separate the fields, and the multiplicity of trees, add greatly to the beauty of the scenery.

We passed through many districts abounding in manufacturing establishments, with their tall chimneys emitting volumes of smoke. While at Rugby, we thought of the noble Doctor Arnold, who has made that place so famous, and of Tom Brown, who has so gracefully recorded his school-days there. We are now in pleasant quarters in the west end of London, and are living as comfortably and quietly as if we were in our own house. Our waiter looks so ministerial in his white cravat, and serves us with an air of such thorough "respectability," that if it were necessary to address a note to him, I should be quite tempted to commence it in the prescribed clerical way, "Reverend Sir."

The annual "May meetings" in Exeter Hall are an institution of London, and we were much interested, the day after our arrival, in attending the anniversary of the British and Foreign Bible Society, to which two American clergymen were delegates. Lord Shaftsbury was in the chair. The Bishops of London and Carlisle spoke very earnestly, and we were glad to hear our dear friend, Dr. F. loudly applauded when he said emphatically, "There is power enough in Protestant truth any time, and anywhere, to conquer Romanism. I am sure I cannot mistake the sentiment of every true Britain, as I know I do not mistake the sentiment of every true American, when I say, an open field, a fair fight, and God help the right!" Lord Shaftsbury's earnest words about America, and the strong desire that there should never be anything but peace between his land and ours, seemed to express the wish of the entire audience.

We have had a pleasant evening with Mrs. Ranyard, who has been so useful among the poor in London, and whose books "The Missing Link," and "The Book and its Story," have given so much information and pleasure. From a little work which she gave us, called "London, and Ten Years Work in it," we learn how wonderful has been the success of the Bible women in teaching the poor and degraded the best and most useful kind of knowledge, the way to help themselves.

As we passed through a part of the famous St. Giles, on our way to Mrs. R.'s, we saw, even yet, an amount of squalid poverty which was sickening. The contrast between *it* and the splendor and display at the Queen's drawing-room the next day, was very striking.

There were superb equipages, gay liveries, footmen and coachmen, generally four on a carriage, with bouquets large enough for breast-plates; beautiful women sparkling with diamonds, and everything else that wealth and rank can give. The Prince of Wales was attended by a troop of horsemen, the band playing "God save the King," and his coachmen and footmen fairly *gleamed* with gold lace. He bowed very pleasantly to the crowd, and *looks* like an amiable young man, whatever he may be in reality. In the midst of all this elegance, we were much surprised at the freedom of a well-dressed man, who walked past the carriages of my Lord This, and my Lady That, exclaiming at the top of his voice, "All this comes out of *our* pockets. O, yes, *we* pay for all this." Although he uttered this many times, no notice was taken of it by the host of policemen who were standing about, to keep order, and he was allowed to pass unmolested.

The people are quite delighted that the Queen is again appearing in public, and crowds were assembled to see her on her way to lay the foundation stone of a new hospital, the day following the drawing-room reception. She was in an open barouche, with the Princess Christian by her side, and the pretty little Princess Beatrice, with her long golden hair floating in crimps over her shoulders, seated in front of her. Prince Leopold made a very handsome Scotch laddie in his Tartan dress. The Queen, in her simple black bonnet, bowed constantly to the right and left, but the expression of her face was decidedly sad, and there was no smile.

After the royal procession had passed, we went to Mortlake, a few miles from London, where we had been invited to lunch with a charming family, whose names are associated with the best and noblest of the land. Near their pleasant place are the grounds formerly belonging to Sir William Temple, where Dean Swift passed so much of his early life. After luncheon an excursion was made to Hampton Court, by way of Bushy Park. We walked a mile through an avenue of horse-chestnut trees, which were one mass of white blossoms, and the effect was very beautiful.

The grounds at Hampton Court are kept in such exquisite order, and the Palace itself so curious and quaint in its architecture, that it could not fail to interest us extremely. The building occupies eight acres of ground, and in order to see it, and its beautiful lawns and gardens, one must walk several miles. The situation is very lovely, being upon the banks of the Thames, and so elevated that the view of the Surrey Hills, and the surrounding country, is very fine. The river itself,

> "At every winding, as the waters run,
> Presents a mirror to the shining sun."

It is not surprising that Henry the Eighth should have asked the ambitious Cardinal Wolsey, who designed the magnificent structure for himself, what were his "intentions in building a palace that far surpassed any of the royal palaces of England?" There was more *tact* than *truth* in his reply, that he was only trying to form a residence worthy of so great a monarch. Whether this great monarch (great in talent, and great in wickedness) desired the gift, or not, it became his, and was afterwards associated with royalty, for many years, and in many ways.

The good "boy-king," Edward the Sixth, was born at Hampton Court, and in sixteen hundred and twenty-five, Charles the First and Queen Henrietta retreated there to avoid the plague then raging in London. Less than twenty years after, their majesties again fled there for refuge from a calamity still more fatal—a calamity which ended in bringing King Charles to the scaffold.

The splendid Gothic Hall designed by Wolsey, and finished by Henry the Eighth, is very magnificent. It is more than a hundred feet long, and sixty high, the roof being most elaborately carved and decorated with the arms and badges of Henry the Eighth. It was used as a theatre during the reign of Elizabeth, and tradition says that some of the plays of Shakspeare were first acted here. We went through long suites of rooms, once the scenes of magnificent banquets and grand Christmas festivals, where we saw hundreds of historical pictures, and portraits of various kings, queens, and persons of highest rank. The sweet face of Mrs. Delaney, the pet of good Queen Charlotte, and the beloved of all who knew her, interested us very much. There is no end to the portraits of George the Third and his numerous offspring, and one wonders that they had patience to sit so frequently for their effigies. It must have furnished our countryman, Benjamin West, the favorite painter of his majesty, an abundance of employment.

Hampton Court has not for a long time been occupied as a royal residence, and there are several suites of apartments in which private families are allowed to reside, by special permission. Through the kindness of the present Queen, it was first thrown open to the public, and the humblest as well as the proudest of her subjects, can now enjoy its various treasures.

We have been several times to Westminster Abbey, and it is impossible to describe the almost overpowering emotions with which one sees this pile, so vast and grand, and so full of historical associations. It becomes more and more wonderful on each succeeding visit. We entered at the "Poets' Corner," where are simple monuments to "rare Ben Johnson," Spenser, Milton, Gray, Dryden, Chaucer, Goldsmith, Addison, Sheridan &c. As I found myself by a simple slab in the pavement, with the words, "David Garrick," carved upon it, I involuntarily looked up to a little gallery where, some years ago, a group of weeping friends stood (Hannah More among them,) to watch the last sad rites to the most wonderful actor of that or any other age. The whole scene seemed so vivid as I stood there, but all who witnessed it have long since passed away. It was with feelings of both awe and reverence that we went from one monument to another, and read names, and saw deeds recorded with many of which we had been long familiar.

The guide who conducts parties through the chapels (of which there are nine) becomes very tiresome with his sing-song manner, and parrot-like way of giving information. One longs to get rid of him, and linger for hours, instead of being hurried on in such a summary manner. In Henry the Seventh's chapel, which has an exquisite carved stone ceiling, and is very beautiful architecturally, the monument of Mary Queen of Scots is seen ; a recumbent statue with a face very lovely, although of stone. Her cousin Elizabeth, in the royal robes and immense ruff in which she delighted, is in another aisle of the same chapel. The tomb of Henry the Seventh himself, said by Lord Bacon to be "one of the stateliest and daintiest in Europe," is in the centre of the chapel. There are effigies in solid brass of Henry and Elizabeth his queen, lying side by side, on a block of black marble. The tomb is placed on a pedestal of black marble, five feet high, and beautifully adorned with brass ornaments. The remains of Edward the Sixth are deposited at the head of this tomb.

In St. Edward's chapel, the uncomfortable looking coronation chair is kept, which has been used from the days of Edward Second to Queen Victoria. Underneath it is the rough sandstone on which all the old kings of Scotland were crowned. The chair is covered with crimson velvet on coronation days, and it is hoped, slightly cushioned, or the old adage would become true, "Uneasy rests the head that wears a crown."

As we wandered about among the many grand and costly monuments, and came at last to the simple flagstones with the letters W. P., and C. J. F. carved upon them, we thought of the enthusiasm of the eccentric John Randolph, who exclaimed on seeing them, "Here lie, side by side, the remains of the two great rivals, William Pitt, and Charles James Fox, whose memory so completely lives in history. No marble monuments are necessary to mark the spot where *their* bodies repose. There is more simple grandeur in those few letters than in all the surrounding monuments, sir!"

We were very fortunate in having tickets to an evening service in Westminster Abbey, which was brilliantly lighted for the occasion—an unusual circumstance. The Archbishop of York preached in behalf of the Church Missionary Society, and the service was choral, closing with the Hallelujah Chorus of Handel, which was performed magnificently, and sounded grander than ever in that grand old pile, which is also the last resting-place of the glorious musician himself.

We went one day to Westminster Hall, once a banqueting hall, and the scene of mirth and revelry for centuries. It is a Gothic apartment, and the largest room in the world unsupported by pillars. The roof is of wood with flying arches, and curious carving. Charles the First was tried and condemned in this hall. Warren Hastings was also tried, and fortunately acquitted here, and at a still later day, it was the scene of George the Fourth's coronation banquet. We were shown through the House of Commons and House of Lords by a very well-dressed, gentlemanly looking man, to whom we hesitated about offering a shilling, but he took it with wonderful ease, and did not seem in the least embarrassed. In fact, it is quite surprising to meet with so many people who are ready to receive a fee, from a penny upward. One need not shrink from offering it under any circumstances.

In the House of Lords, the Lord Chancellor was holding court, surrounded by lawyers in their large curly wigs, which nearly extinguished them. Everything was done in the most quiet, orderly manner possible. Sir Roundell Palmer, the former attorney-general, made an argument, which was listened to very eagerly by the black-gowned, big wigs, present, as well as by those of us who were only allowed a peep at the dignitaries from a quiet corner.

The new Houses of Parliament are very magnificent and beautiful, the style being richly decorated Gothic. They are divided into numerous apartments, courts, passages and halls. Some of the latter are immense, and adorned with statuary, and busts of eminent statesmen. The House of Lords is perfectly gorgeous in gilt mouldings, stained glass windows, paintings, velvet, and everything else essential to comfort and grandeur. The letters V. R. occur so frequently that a gifted countrywoman of ours once suggested that it must mean "very ridiculous."

The House of Commons is more simple, but very elegant, notwithstanding, and one could not but feel that so much show and display were quite unnecessary to grave legislation.

No one can come to London without paying a visit to Madame Toussaud's wax-works, and we were extremely amused with this "calm and classical" collection, so full of the "unchanging air of coldness and gentility," which Mrs. Jarley so much admired. It becomes very confusing at last, particularly when one turns about to make an humble apology for stumbling against a lady in the crowd, and discovers that the lady is "looking intensely nowhere, and staring with extraordinary earnestness at nothing," and is really only a "figger."

A gentleman of our party who is full of humor, but generally looks very grave and wise, seated himself in the centre of a long lounge, to rest, while we went to see Napoleon's travelling carriage, his son's crib, and some other relics; to say nothing of the dreadful guillotine. While sitting there, a young girl came up to our dignified friend, and surveyed him from top to toe, evidently admiring the grave old gentleman very much, and wondering why he was not labelled like the rest; when he suddenly gave her a look brimming over with fun, and she scampered off half frightened out of her wits. We were very much amused with an amiable-looking old gentleman, with spectacles on his nose, who was watching a group of royal personages, and occupied the best seat in front of them, in order to do so. He turned his head from side to side, occasionally, as if he were quite bent upon seeing everything, and we were beginning to think it was time he had resigned his place to some one else, when a closer inspection showed us that his powers of locomotion were of a very limited kind. The feeling after one first discovers that the individual near you, instead of being flesh and blood, is only a *sham*, is very peculiar.

St. Paul's Cathedral, situated as it is, in the very heart of London, and in its most crowded neighborhood, is blackened with coal smoke, and looks like anything but white marble, of which it is built. It is a massive pile, and when one is underneath the dome, its real grandeur impresses itself very forcibly. The choir, with its rich oak carvings of festoons of flowers, scrolls, fruits and figures, is very beautiful. Christopher Wren, the famous architect, laid the corner stone himself in sixteen hundred and seventy-five, and lived to see his son deposit the highest stone upon the cupola, thirty-five years after. His remains are beneath a plain slab in the crypt, but a Latin inscription in the choir above, says, "Beneath, lies Sir Christopher Wren, the builder of this church, who lived upwards of ninety years, not for himself, but for the public good. Reader, seekest thou his monument? Look around!"

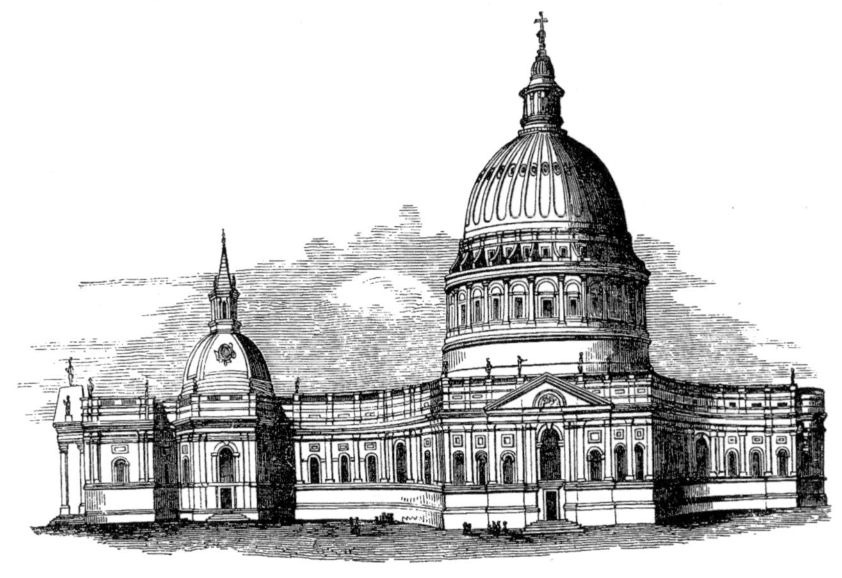

ST. PAUL'S CATHEDRAL.

It is an interesting fact that the first statue erected in St Paul's, was that of the great lexicographer, Dr. Johnson. There are a great many monuments to the memory of distinguished men—among them, John Howard the philanthropist, who is represented trampling on fetters and chains, with a key in one hand, and a scroll in the other, inscribed, "Plea for the Improvement of Prisons." One cannot but look with reverence on even the sculptured form of a man so truly benevolent and good. England's two greatest heroes are lying in the crypt of the cathedral. Lord Nelson is placed immediately under the centre of the dome, in a black marble sarcophagus, having on it a coronet and cushion. It has a granite foundation, and only the simple inscription, "Horatio, Viscount Nelson." In a chamber near by, is the superb tomb of the Duke of Wellington, made from one block of porphyry, highly polished, which weighed originally more than seventy tons. It has a foundation of red granite, about four feet high, and at each corner is sculptured the head of a sleeping lion, also in granite. At the four corners of the vault are gas jets, rising through red granite shafts. The immense funeral car, drawn, at that time, by twelve horses, and wrought from cannon captured in different battles under the "Iron Duke," is in another chamber. It is covered with black velvet, fringed with silver, and six wooden horses, looking as much like life as a painted horse can, and wearing the sombre trappings used at the funeral, are attached to the car.

Certainly, England has not been wanting in any honor that could be conferred upon the conqueror of Napoleon, both in life and death.

Our visit to Sydenham Palace, which occurred on a lovely day, was made very interesting through the kindness of the family of the distinguished naturalist, Mr. Waterhouse Hawkins, who has placed so many of the remarkable restored animals about the beautiful grounds. There are thirty, or more, of these creatures, once inhabitants of England and Ireland, but now extinct. Some of them are enormous, and one can but rejoice that they belong to the "things that were."

The Palace is a marvellous structure, and contains a little of everything. One can walk for hours through its floors and galleries, examining the wonderful collections of treasures brought from all parts of the world. There are copies of many of the most celebrated works of art—courts arranged to represent different nations, and adorned with statuary—such as the Egyptian court—the Grecian—the Roman—the Pompeian, &c. Then there are models of ships, bridges, and machinery, and specimens of the animal and mineral productions of all countries.

In the tropical gardens, there are exquisite flowers and shrubs, and even trees, growing. Indeed, flowers and fountains meet you everywhere, and the whole light airy structure seems like fairy-land. The situation is commanding, and the grounds beautifully arranged with a profusion of statues, grottoes and fountains. We were present at a grand concert given by the Handel Society, underneath the great central dome of the building, and the music sounded magnificently there.

The next evening we heard music of quite another character at the Baptist Tabernacle church in Southwark, which, although less artistic, was none the less impressive. There the whole congregation seemed to sing as one voice, the pastor setting them the example by singing with all his might and main himself. It was really grand. Mr. Spurgeon's church is in the midst of a densely populated portion of the city. The interior of the building is oval in shape, and there are double galleries running around the whole church. It is well lighted and ventilated.

The congregation was immense, filling every part of the enormous structure. As each person entered, a small envelope was given him, or her, with a request printed upon it that contributions be placed in it, and deposited in boxes at the doors, for the benefit of the college which is preparing young men for the ministry. In this way, two hundred dollars, sometimes more, are collected every Sunday, mostly in pennies. The church seats about five thousand, and besides those who were seated, hundreds stood during the entire service.

Through the politeness of one of the officials, we were very kindly placed in excellent seats in the first gallery, very near to, and almost on a level with the pulpit. Precisely at half-past six, Mr. Spurgeon entered, and took his seat on a small platform, projecting from the second gallery. He is short, rather stout, and young in his appearance. There is nothing to indicate the wonderful power he has as a preacher.

The services commenced with a short prayer, which was somewhat characteristic. He asked that our thoughts might not be "gadding about" during the service, and implored blessings on "Mary and Sarah, and Willie and Thomas, and the little baby whose voice we had just heard." After the prayer, a hymn was given out, verse by verse—then followed the reading and expounding of a portion of Scripture—then a long prayer, and singing again. The sermon was upon the verses of Balaam's prophecy, in which the Saviour is set forth under the figure of a star. He made seven heads. First, the star represented dominion. Second, shining. Third, guidance. Fourth, constancy. Fifth, influence. Sixth, wonder. Seventh, glory. It was a plain, earnest, practical presentation of the offices of Christ, which a child could have understood. The vast audience listened with breathless attention, throughout, and we all felt interested and edified. It could not have been called a scholarly or finished sermon, but Christ was faithfully and fully preached.

With a good delivery, fresh and practical thoughts, and with homely, yet pertinent illustrations, he is enabled to keep the attention of his hearers to the end. His exhortations and applications are interspersed throughout the whole discourse, and not left to the close. The concluding service was a hymn, and a short prayer, with benediction. The whole service was something to be seen and remembered, as among the most remarkable things of this wonderful metropolis, and we cannot soon forget it.

We spent a pleasant day at Hampstead, where our lovely friend Mrs. N. resides, in B—— Lodge, a charming spot, with a pretty garden and lawn. I made my début upon a donkey, while there, as there were scores of these creatures upon the heath,

"All saddled and bridled and ready for fight,"

which their various owners urged upon us in the most hospitable manner. Having long been desirous of trying one of these shaggy, long, eared beasts, I selected a particularly amiable-looking animal, and mounted—but alas!

"*I* knowed a donkey, wot wouldn't go,"

at least, not in the right direction, for although

the owner punched him with a stick, and screamed in his great ears loud enough to deafen him, he persisted in trying both sides of the road at once, and made such desperate aim for the ditches, that like many another debutante, I was seized with "stage fright," and retreated in the most ignominious manner. The views from the highest point of Hampstead Heath quite repaid us for our long walk, and I did not regret parting with my gay deceiver. As we were returning through the lanes, and quaint old streets, we passed a plain brick house, covered with ivy, standing on the brow of a hill, overlooking the town. There was a look of elegance and refinement about it which we felt ought to belong to the residence of the author of the "Schonberg Cotta Family," whose home it is.

Our next expedition was to the Zoological Gardens of Regents Park, which are wonderfully perfect in their arrangements. The animals are not cramped up in miserable little cages, where they keep walking up and down, looking very fierce and forlorn. On the contrary, many of them have a beautiful little cottage to live in, surrounded by a high, open fence; and then they have pools of clear, pure water, in which they bathe, and they really seem so comfortable and happy, that it is a pleasure to look at them.

The gardens are so beautifully laid out, that we were not surprised to see many happy families there, consisting of fathers and mothers, children and nurses, who evidently had come for the entire day, with capacious lunch-baskets. It is pleasant to see so many of the lovely parks and gardens here, free to all, and very delightful to see how numerous are those green spots in this great city.

It is "the season" in London just now; Parliament being in session, and all the fashionable world congregating here, so that everything is in its best and most attractive dress. We never tire of the beautiful parks, which in the afternoon are thronged with elegant equipages, ladies on horseback galloping up and down Rotton Row, and pedestrians enjoying the gay scene. The pretty children on ponies scarcely larger than a Newfoundland dog, led by a groom, and with a nurse walking at their side, we always watched with peculiar pleasure. One day, however, our delight in these scenes received a shock from which it was difficult to recover, when we saw the horse of a young gentleman become perfectly unmanageable and rush madly along the bridle path, while its rider made the most desperate efforts to keep the saddle. When we saw him at last dashed to the ground, and his poor lifeless body extended on the grass shortly afterwards, we felt that a ride in Rotton Row was dearly paid for in this case.

Kensington Gardens, at the western extremity of Hyde Park, are nearly a mile square, and are very beautiful. There are glorious old trees in the grounds, and in some places it was like being in a vast forest, far away from the "busy haunts of men." We seated ourselves on some iron chairs, near a pretty lake, in front of Kensington Palace, to enjoy the scene and partake of a little lunch, when a very young gentleman with a police decoration on his cap, came to demand a fee for the chairs, which in the innocence of our hearts, we thought some benevolent person had placed there "pro bono publico." While we willingly paid the demand, we were again struck with the many ways of obtaining money. A boy will chase a cab for a mile, to open the door for you, and feel liberally rewarded for his polite attention if you give him a penny. Probably these little jobs are all he has to depend upon. Kensington Palace is a very unpretending brick building, but interesting from having been the abode of royalty for two centuries.

More than thirty years ago, a young girl of eighteen, who then resided there with her mother, was awakened in the night and told that the Archbishop of Canterbury desired an interview; her uncle William the Fourth having just died. She hastily attired herself and met the venerable prelate. He informed her of her accession to the throne, and in deep agitation, her first words were, "I ask your prayers in my behalf." They knelt down together, and thus the young sovereign inaugurated her reign. How well she has fulfilled the trust reposed in her, up to the present hour, we all know, for certainly no Queen has better deserved the devotion of her loving subjects, than the excellent Queen Victoria.

We are about to leave England for a season, and we do so with much regret, for

> "O, England! full of years, yet passing fair,
> I drink thy beauty with a child's delight."

Paris, May 19.

The dreaded Channel has been passed, and like many another "uncertain evil," it has proved only imaginary. We were two hours crossing from Dover to Calais, and scarcely a ripple could be seen on the surface of the water. The trip was really most charming, and we all felt that the Channel had been undeservedly abused. We could not but wonder, however, what travellers were expected to do, in case of the storms which are so frequent on that sea, when the accommodations of the steamer were so very limited. How such boats on such a thoroughfare can be tolerated, is certainly most remarkable. At Calais our luggage was seized upon by men in blue blouses, who rushed up two pairs of high steps, which were covered with a green slippery slime; for the tide was low, and the dock, which ought to have been underneath the water, was now standing out in bold relief. On reaching the top, we were ushered into a bedlam, known generally as a custom-house, where we fully realized the sage remark of Thomas Hood, that "even the children in France speak French." The custom-house officers were very polite, and believed us when we answered "*rien*," without investigating very closely. So we were soon on our way again, and were rather glad to know that the country about Calais was marshy and bleak, for we were almost immediately enveloped in such a cloud of dust, that it was impossible to see anything. *Such* dust I think I never encountered before, and we were not sorry when at the end of six hours we found ourselves in bright, cheerful Paris, at the most comfortable Hotel de L'Athénée. Our stay will not be long just now, but we have indulged in a bit of gayety in the shape of a visit to the Cirque de l'imperatrice, where we saw wonderful riding, beautiful horses, and a building of vast dimensions, most tastefully arranged. The French clowns, even when they do not *say* anything, are so exquisitely funny in their *actions*, that one cannot help being amused, and we laughed very heartily at their various antics.

The Hotel des Invalides interested us extremely, and we were glad to see the hundreds of old and infirm soldiers there so kindly cared for. A few are still left who fought under the first Napoleon, and who remember him with affectionate reverence. We were shown the kitchen, dining-hall, and library, and were allowed to enter the old church, which in Napoleon's day was adorned with nearly three thousand flags. Underneath the Dome des Invalides is the superb tomb of Napoleon, in a circular excavation many feet deep. The floor is composed of laurels formed in mosaic, from the centre of which rises the reddish brown granite sarcophagus, which is surrounded by twelve colossal figures, emblematic of victory. At the entrance of the vault are the words from Napoleon's will, in which he asks that his ashes may repose upon the borders of the Seine, in the midst of the French people whom he has so much loved. We could not but be glad that his last wish was gratified.

The famous Bois de Boulogne has been enchanting in this bright weather, and we enjoyed its miles of lovely drives exceedingly. We found it thronged with carriages of every description, and all the elegance of Paris seemed to be in them. The beautiful cascades and lakes are so like nature, that one can scarcely believe they have been arranged by the hand of art, and that the rocks are not real rocks, formed by a higher power than man. The Vacherie, with its fifty handsome cows, delighted us very much. It is surrounded by beautiful grounds, and there are tables at which persons can sit and partake of the innocent luxury of fresh milk. It was served in small white china bowls, and the pretty picturesque costume of the young waiting maids, and their pleasant manners, added greatly to the charm. Many occupants of the carriages ordered the milk to be brought to them there, and enjoyed it at their leisure without alighting. We dined with some friends at the Café de Madrid, and were the victims of our cunning cocher, who took us in the most circuitous direction possible, and several times lost his way in order to prolong the expedition. The Café was about ten minutes' drive from the Vacherie, and we were an hour and a half reaching it. However, the place proved so agreeable, and we enjoyed the meeting with dear friends so much, that we soon forgot the slight annoyance. Our excellent dinner was served to us in a lovely shaded bower, in the nicest manner possible, and as the garçon who attended us had lived a few years in our "land of steady habits," he took particular pleasure in bestowing upon us his society and patronage. We asked him if he intended returning to Connecticut, and were not surprised that he said "*no*" very emphatically; for a pleasure-loving Frenchman must find our busy, working land very dull.

Paris has quite reminded us of home, in the building which we see going on in all directions, and in the tearing down of many places already built. The throngs in the streets are incessant, and we have looked with wonder at the dexterity with which men on velocipedes have managed to rush by vehicle after vehicle, and shape their course between and among them, without in any way interfering with their speed, or endangering themselves.

Genoa, May 22.

We are thus far on our way to the "Eternal City," having left Paris on the morning of the nineteenth. The country was most interesting during the entire day, being through Burgundy, with its beautiful vineyards, and rows upon rows of poplar-trees, with an occasional sprinkling of the morus multicaulis.

At Dijon, the conductor announced that we should remain twenty-eight minutes, and as we were informed that there was an excellent table d'hôte at the station, we decided to try it. We were shown into a large pleasant room, with neat muslin curtains at the eight windows. The table-cloth was as white as snow, and the napkins, ditto. We had seven different courses, with changes of plates at each course. Soup, roast beef with potatoes, lamb and spinach, pickled fish, asparagus, roast chicken and salad, pudding, followed by coffee, cheese, and fruit. Everything was beautifully served, without bustle or confusion ; and of course there was a profusion of Burgundy wine, there being three bottles placed before each plate. There were also at intervals in the centre of the table, circular shelves in pyramidal form, which were filled with bottles. All this was furnished for a little more than four francs each person. Shall we ever see the time in our own land when a meal can be eaten so comfortably at a railway station?

Six o'clock the next morning found us very near Marseilles, crossing a dreary flat, composed of stones and high grass, with a decidedly saltish atmosphere prevailing. We were glad to refresh ourselves at a comfortable hotel, after our night in the cars, and afterwards we drove about the city. From a bare, rocky hill, called Notre Dame de la Garde, from the curious chapel on the summit, we

MARSEILLES.

had a fine view of Marseilles itself, which is spread over a gradually sloping basin, and surrounded by hills covered with vineyards, and olive gardens, among the bleak-looking rocks. On the other side, the beautiful blue Mediterranean stretches far off in the distance. The chapel of "La bonne Mêre," is in so elevated a situation, that the ascent to it cannot be made without much panting and many pauses, but it is a great resort. An image of the Virgin, carved in olive wood, and of great antiquity, is held in the highest veneration throughout the Mediterranean by sailors and fishermen and their families, who bestow offerings of all kinds to propitiate her favor. At every convenient place in the ascent, we found women stationed with candles, medals, and rosaries, which they urged us to buy, and which we respectfully declined doing. Our stay in Marseilles was rather brief, but quite satisfactory, and we had a charming expedition to Nice on the same day, by the railway which skirts along the sea-shore. The scenery much of the time was very grand, and we passed Toulon with its strongly fortified harbor, Cannes, and other favorite winter watering-places.

At Cannes, Lord Brougham, full of years and

honors, had died a short time before at his pretty villa, named Louise Eleonore. Nice, with its surrounding mountains to shut out the cold winds from the glorious sea at the south, must be a delicious winter climate. The temperature is soft and mild, and flowers are in blossom all the year round in the open air—while there are orange trees in every stage, from the blossom to the mature fruit. The town is almost deserted now, and it was with difficulty that we found a hotel prepared to take us in. The "Hotel de France" at length opened its hospitable doors, and we found it pleasantly situated and well kept. The next morning we drove to the old chateau, a very high point which is reached by a road, *en zigzag*, and from which we had a glorious view of the city, the Mediterranean, and the spurs of the Alps in the distance.

We are in the midst of tropical fruits and flowers, and constantly see the most brilliant geraneums growing wild in great profusion. The single scarlet poppy seems to be the *weed* of the country, and we see millions of them in the fields, and by the roadside, making everything look very gay. When we left Nice, I carried in my hand a branch containing seven oranges, which I had picked in the garden of the hotel. Our sail of eight hours, from Nice to Genoa, was delightful. The sea was perfectly calm, and we kept near the shore, thus having a good view of the mountains, the various towns, and the marvellous Cornice road, which follows the indentations of the shore, now ascending, and then descending high mountains, and then appearing again along the beach.

We have spent a part of two days in wandering about Genoa, which is well called "La Superba" from its commanding position upon the Bay, and the magnificence of its palaces and churches. The streets in nearly all parts of the town, however, are very narrow, and as there are no sidewalks, the middle of the street is as much used by pedestrians as any other part. The long white scarf which the women arrange so gracefully about their heads, and which falls in light folds over their necks and arms, is very picturesque, and gives a softness to the plainest face.

From the church of Sante Maria di Carrignano, we had a perfect view of the city with its superb situation ; and the church itself, a fine building of black and white marble, is one of great interest. It was built at a great expense by the Saulis family, who also erected a grand bridge over a dry chasm, in order to make the church accessible. It has some very fine pictures and statuary, among them a martydom by Carlo Maratti, which is very striking.

In one of the public squares stands the beautiful monument erected to the memory of Columbus, whom the Genoese are proud to claim as their son. Columbus stands tall and erect, with an earnest expression of face, his hand resting upon an anchor, while a female figure, representing America, is kneeling and looking up at him. The base of the monument bears this inscription :

A
CHRISTOFERO COLOMBO.
LA PATRIA.

An ancient house near by is pointed out as one in which Columbus once lived. We drove out to the famous Pallavicini villa, which is about five miles from the city. Everything that taste and wealth combined *can* do, has been done to make this place most charming. There are fountains, cascades, summer-houses, grottos, statues, exquisite flowers, and rare trees. In one of the grottos we entered a boat, and were rowed through narrow passages, formed of stalactites, and on coming out again at another side, we found ourselves surrounded by banks of flowers, and floating on a beautiful little lake. There is a constant succession of surprises about the grounds, and when one enters an attractive summer-house, and receives a jet of water, fine as spray, from an unseen source, the surprise is decidedly startling. The whole scene was exquisite, and one felt like lingering there a longer time than the guide was disposed to give. Our drive back to Genoa, over a dusty road, was not a pleasant exchange for this Paradise.

Florence, May 28.

The morning after our departure from Genoa found us in Leghorn, where we landed from the steamer in a small boat, and were received by the dreadful clatter of an Italian crowd, who insisted on seizing every parcel, ourselves included, and bestowed attentions upon us which we would gladly have dispensed with. Fortunately the custom-house officers manifested less interest in us and our possessions, and let us off very easily.

We made ourselves quite at home at the "Victory and Washington Hotel," names we are accustomed to associate together, and after breakfast sallied forth in search of whatever might interest us in in this bustling seaport town. The principal result of our expedition was the purchase of a Leghorn hat, which we bought in the usual dishonest Italian way, by offering the man just half the sum he asked for it. As it was all it was worth, we were not surprised that he should have taken it, but we did not admire the principle of the thing very much.

We were not disposed to linger long in Leghorn, and were soon on our way to Pisa, where the Leaning Tower, the Cathedral, the Baptistry, and the Campo Santo, form a splendid group of buildings. The Leaning Tower certainly does lean fearfully, and it will probably always remain a point in dispute, whether the inclination was intentional or not, as it has now been six centuries in this position. At the top of the tower are the bells, to contain which it was erected. They vary in size, but are all large and heavy, and are always rung at funerals.

The Cathedral is very old and grand, and among its wonderful contents, we looked with much interest at the large antique bronze lamp, suspended from the ceiling, which first suggested to Galileo the theory of the pendulum, nearly three hundred years ago. The high altar of the

Cathedral is very large, and elaborately ornamented, and there are some very fine paintings of Andrea del Sarto.

The Baptistry is very beautiful, being almost entirely of marble ; but there is a look of desolation about it when one first enters, as the space is wide and high, and only broken by the font and pulpit. The latter is exquisitely carved, and supported by seven columns, composed of different marbles, which rest upon the crouching figures of animals. There is a very remarkable echo in the Baptistry, and the really musical voice of our guide was repeated again and again in the most sonorous manner, as he sang in loud tones to call out the response.

The Campo Santo is composed of cloisters, lined with curious old frescoes, and within these cloisters is the sacred earth brought from Jerusalem in twelve hundred and twenty-eight. Most of the tombs are very curious and old, many of them very elaborately sculptured and adorned with statuary. There are some modern tombs among them, for burials take place here still, occasionally ; and among the recent monuments we saw one to Count Cavour, the great statesman and benefactor of Italy.

We drove past the Palazzo Lanfranchini, prettily situated on the Arno, in which Lord Byron lived some time, and where he wrote some of his most famous and most wicked poems. The railway from Pisa was through a most charming, cultivated country, which becomes more and more beautiful the nearer it approaches Florence. Now, as I write, I hear the rushing of the waters of the Arno, in front of the hotel, and although truth compels me to say that the river looks decidedly muddy and yellow at this season of the year, yet it *is* the Arno, and we are in Firenze la Bella! What treasures have we already laid up in the way of paintings and sculpture! How impossible ever to forget them, and yet how impossible to describe them.

The first look at the Pitti Palace suggests a prison, so abundant are the iron bars, and so rough the walls. One can hardly imagine the feelings of the dying Medici, who replied to the priest, when he was describing to him the heavenly joys upon which he was about to enter: "But *I* am content with the Pitti Palace." When once within, however, it is not difficult to understand his entire satisfaction. We were shown through the elegant private apartments of

King Victor Emanuel, looking out upon the Boboli gardens, which are a profusion of terraces, and adorned with flowers, statuary, and fountains, an exquisite picture in themselves. Then the pictures within! What a feeling of *possession* it gives one to see the Madonna della Seggiola of Raphael, the Virgin and Child of Murillo, the Bella Donna and Magdalen of Titian, and hundreds of others, of which one has heard, and seen in prints so many, many times. We wandered for hours, drinking in all these pleasures with a delight that never wearied.

From the Pitti Palace we went to the Uffizi Gallery by means of a long corridor, or covered bridge, which takes one over the Arno, and is hung the greater part of the way with tapestry. With very little delay, we sought the "Tribune," in the centre of which stands the far-famed Venus de Medici, beautiful in form and extremely graceful, but without the *soul* in her face which one would like to see. Near her, hang the Madonna del Cordellino, La Fornarini, and St. John Preaching in the Desert, by Raphael, and a Madonna and Child by Andrea del Sarto. Each one a gem, of which one could never tire.

The device of Florence, a rose in a field of

lilies, seems a very appropriate one, situated as she is in a theatre of verdant hills, covered with vines and olives, and dotted with villas. There is a constant fascination about life here, and one cannot but feel that ample provision is made for harmless enjoyments—enjoyments which cultivate and refine. Pictures, statues, music, flowers, seem a part of the place itself. The drive to the Cascine is a never-failing source of attraction, and for two or three hours of an afternoon, all Florence can be seen, walking or driving along the banks of the Arno, underneath the magnificent trees, or stopping near the Grand Duke's farm-house to listen to the band. This is the great gathering point, and carriages draw up side by side, for the inmates to converse—flower-girls in picturesque costume, dash rashly in among the horses, to offer you their fragrant bouquets—ladies on horseback, attended by officers in full uniform, add to the beauty of the scene, while children with their nurses are made happy by a ramble in the woods, or by the river-side. A gayer scene it is scarcely possible to imagine. Even the coachmen, it is said, partake of this elegance, and in case of any disturbance among themselves, classically call upon Venus or Bacchus, or swear "by the aspect of Minerva!" This I cannot vouch for, not having been the witness of any such contention.

It is pleasant to know that in the midst of all this gayety, so much is being done to instruct and elevate, by means of religious teaching and literature. The orphan asylum and public schools, under the care of an Italian Protestant, are very successful; while the Bible, and various religious works published by the Italian Evangelical Publication Society, are circulated with a freedom which a few years ago would have been deemed impossible.

We have enjoyed meeting Mr. Powers, the sculptor, of whom all Americans are proud, and it was a great pleasure to be conducted about his studio by him. We regarded the long apron and closely-fitting linen cap, as becoming articles of dress on *him*, and his fine eyes glowed with feeling as he spoke of his native land. The Greek Slave, long so familiar to us, looked more beautiful than ever, by the side of her master, and we saw many exquisite busts and statues—among them the busts of our countrymen Edward Everett, Robert C. Winthrop, and Doctor Bellows—all of which were wonderfully like the originals.

I could not but think, as I stood there, of the little Kentucky boy, the son of a United States Senator, who on his return from Louisville, where he had been to see the Greek Slave, fell from the cars between Frankfort and Lexington, and his arm was so terribly crushed that it had to be amputated. When his weeping mother went to his bedside, shortly after the operation was over, and said to him, "My poor boy, your visit to Louisville has been a dear one to you." "Ah, mother," replied the little fellow, with a look and tone of animation, "but I *saw the Greek Slave.*" It is not strange that Mr. Powers should have been touched by such a tribute to his genius, and he expressed a strong desire to know the fate of the heroic boy. It is more than thirty years since Mr. Powers has seen his native country, yet he is enthusiastically American, and has honored us abroad, not only by his works, but in his pure, spotless life—a life quiet and unostentatious, but full of love and charity to all.

We visited the house in which Michael Angelo lived and died—it is quaint and old-fashioned, but the apartments are quite spacious and elegant. They are kept very nearly as they were in the days of the wonderfully gifted artist, and many of his sketches hang upon the walls, with other works of art—among them portraits of Dante, Petrarch, and other celebrated men of Tuscany. In a little cabinet where he used to write, are preserved his sword and cane, and a pair of slippers which he wore more than three hundred years ago. We felt as if the genius of the place must be *near*, on seeing these things of every-day use.

A house not less interesting to us was one with a marble slab inserted in the wall, telling the passers-by that here lived and wrote Elizabeth Barrett Browning—the Casa Guidi which she has immortalized in her grand poem. We afterwards went to the beautiful cemetery, where a sculptured sarcophagus, with only the letters E. B. B. inscribed upon it, shows the last resting-place of this truly great and noble woman. How touching seemed her own lines, as we stood there :

> And, friends !—dear friends !—when it shall be
> That this low breath has gone from me,
> And round my bier ye come to weep,
> Let one, most loving of you all,
> Say "Not a tear must o'er her fall,
> 'He giveth his beloved sleep !'"

The Cathedral, with the dome which Michael Angelo so much admired, and the Baptistry with its wonderful bronze doors, are objects of great interest. So, too, is the Santa Croce, with its many monuments to illustrious dead—among them Michael Angelo, Dante, and Galileo. The Medicean Chapel at the San Lorenzo is gorgeous in beautiful marbles, exquisite mosaics and precious stones, the lofty walls being entirely covered with them. The Grand Dukes of Tuscany are glorified in this chapel, their remains lying in the crypt below, while their armorial bearings adorn the walls above, and statuary and cenotaphs denote their rank and wealth. Some of the statues are by Michael Angelo. One, of the Duke of Urbino, in a sitting posture, is very grand. He was the father of Catherine de Medici, who afterwards became the queen of Henry the Second of France, and rendered herself infamous by her persecution of the Huguenots.

Rome.

A lovely moonlight evening found us on our way here, and the night passed so very rapidly that there seemed only a few moments between the announcement of the names of the different towns we passed through. The beautiful, cloudless early morning found us in a country so enchanting that we were glad to unclose our weary eyes and gaze with delight, even after a night of little sleep. The scenery was varied, and comprised every variety of natural beauty—sometimes mountainous, with rugged rocks, then cultivated plains, green slopes, and sheltered valleys. Everywhere we saw a profusion of grape-vines growing in festoons between trees; a graceful arrangement which we had not observed before. We journeyed on through this enchanted land until nearly ten o'clock, when the dome of St. Peter's burst upon our view, and in a few moments more we were in Rome. Rome,

> "The city that so long
> Reigned absolute, the mistress of the world."

When we alighted from the cars a *ruin* met our gaze at once—some magnificent fragments of the baths of Diocletian ; and we felt this to be a proper introduction to the grand old city, although it was rather a sad reminder of past greatness. We drove at once to the Hotel de Londres, on the Piazza di Spagua, where rooms awaited us, with balconied windows looking out upon the square, and within sound of the quaint-looking fountain near by. It was so pleasant to sit there and rest, and realize that we were in Rome, that for some hours we were very quiet. A charming afternoon, however, tempted us to drive to St. Peter's, where we found no words in which to express our admiration and astonishment. The semi-circular colonnades, so familiar to us in pictures, seemed more remarkable still, when we saw that they were supported by four rows of columns, with sufficient room between the inner rows for the passage of two carriages abreast. The fountains, too, as we heard the plashing of the gracefully-falling water, added not a little to the beauty of the entrance to this majestic temple. The interior so completely bewilders one with its splendor and magnificence, that it is impossible for a long time to take it in, or comprehend its magnitude. Marbles, mosaics, pictures, gilding and brilliant colors abound, and one must look again and again before one can appreciate its treasures, or the gigantic scale on which everything is arranged. The bronze canopy,—in itself large enough for a small church,—which covers the high altar, stands beneath the stupendous dome, and underneath the high altar is said to be the grave of St. Peter himself. This altar is only used on solemn occasions, and then

ST. PETER'S.

the Pope officiates. Near by is the celebrated bronze statue of St. Peter, sitting in a chair, with the right foot extended, which has been so often and so lovingly kissed by the faithful that several of the toes have lost their shape. We noticed that some particularly neat persons wiped it off with a clean pocket handkerchief before kissing, while we strongly suspected that most of the devotees did not possess that necessary article ; St. Peter's being open to all ranks and conditions.

Soon after our return to the hotel, two funeral processions passed through the Piazza in front of our windows, consisting of long files of monks in white robes, bearing tapers. Their chanting, which sounded like the most dismal wailing, was anything but exhilarating, and we were not sorry when the doleful psalmody ceased, and the procession disappeared.

Sunday being Whitsunday, we went early to the Sistine Chapel, in the prescribed black dresses and vails, without which no women are admitted, so that we all looked as if we had suddenly gone into mourning. After passing the Swiss Guard, in their curious costumes, composed of red, yellow and black stripes, with white plumes and broad ruffles, we took our places at the entrance, among many others, dressed, like ourselves, in sable garments.

When the doors were opened there was a rush for the best seats, and much pushing and scrambling, quite in the style of a theatrical entertainment. A lively conversation was kept up on all sides, not only until the service commenced, but long after; and we were quite amused with a young English girl who had recently become converted to the Roman Catholic faith, who gossipped and dropped upon her knees, all in one breath.

The ceremonies were very imposing, and the music, at times, very grand. The cardinals, in their red hats, and long scarlet silk gowns, entered one by one. Their trains were tied in a knot until they were in the chapel, when two attendants untied and spread them out several yards upon the floor, in a sadly wrinkled state. We were struck with the remarkably fine faces of many of the cardinals—among them Cardinals Antonelli and Bonaparte—the latter resembling the pictures of the first Napoleon very much. The Pope wore his triple crown, studded with jewels, and was one mass of gold, rich lace, and all kinds of "man millinery." He spoke very distinctly—his strong ringing voice resounding through the chapel with great clearness. Two handsome little Italian boys of eight or ten years of age, superbly dressed in maroon-colored velvet, and who are the Pope's pages, interested us very much with their bright faces and sparkling eyes, and we could not but wonder what the future had in store for them.

When the service was over, a very motley procession wended its way down the staircases and in the colonnade, composed of the Swiss Guard, ladies in black veils, cardinals in bright robes, and priests in every variety of sacerdotal garment. At the foot of the staircase, the superb carriages of the cardinals drove up, with a coachman in full livery upon the box, and three footmen standing up behind, bedecked with velvet and gold embroidery, making a most showy appearance as they dashed rapidly along.

We have made very pleasant visits to some of the studios, and found most of the artists still in Rome, although it is getting late in the season. Mr. Mozier has some exquisite statues—among them the Il Penseroso of Milton, full of dignity and grace; Rebecca at the Well, and the Prodigal Son, which is very expressive and beautiful. A lovely little statue called "Spring," representing a young girl plucking a flower, proved a temptation to one of our party, and he became the fortunate possessor of the fair young creature. In the studio of the poet-painter, Mr. Buchanan Read, we were much interested in a picture called "Sheridan's Ride," which was intended to illustrate his well-known poem. The General's eager, earnest face, full of fire and courage, and the unflinching spirit of his superb horse, are very finely expressed, and the whole painting is life-like and animated.

We found many things in Miss Hosmer's studio to admire—the queenly Zenobia, and the laughing Puck, among them. The statue of Thomas H. Benton, made for the city of St. Louis, is very dignified and grand, although some one has said of it, that the "ideal Benton hangs his head, which the real Benton never did." Miss Hosmer's apartments looked so thoroughly charming, that we were not surprised at the fascination this land of art and song has for her. Mr. Terry had a lovely Marguerite on the easel, and there were also some other gems in his studio, in the way of portraits and historical paintings. In Mr. Rhinehart's studio we found much to delight us, but we were particularly charmed with his Hero—the Hero of Leander. Mr. Charles Francis Adams, our accomplished minister to England, stood quite spell-bound before this exquisitely graceful statue for some time, and we could not but admire his taste.

After enjoying so many specimens of modern art, we paid a visit to the Vatican, where the galleries are so amazing as to defy all description. New splendors open upon you continually, and its treasures are so numerous that no imagination can conceive their wonderful variety. Many of them are world-famous, but it would take a life-time fully to appreciate them all. The Apollo Belvidere standing so exaltant in his triumphant beauty, and the Laocoon so impressive in his dying agony, one can never forget. Equally impossible would it be to forget the Transfiguration, and Madonna di Foligno of Raphael, the Communion of St. Jerome by Domenichino, and many others, which once seen, are forever impressed on the memory.

We have been driving much about Rome, and everywhere we find it intensely interesting.

Some of the streets may be dirty and gloomy, but there is always something to make one forget that they are so, and they are never commonplace. Whichever way you turn a fountain is sure to be playing, for water is as abundant as the light of day itself, and these fountains are in themselves constant objects of pleasure. The ruins of Rome must be seen to be fully comprehended. The Forum with its broken columns; the temples, baths, palaces, and remains of old aqueducts—the Colosseum, vast and grand, which now at the end of eighteen centuries is defying the touch of time. Great care, however, is taken to preserve it as it is, and in many places, new bricks have been inserted to prop the crumbling walls. The arches are very fine, and as one wanders under them, and through the corridors, the deserted look, the intense silence, the drooping vines and grass upon the walls, and the evident disuse, are very striking. It is difficult to feel that those three galleries used to be filled with more than a hundred thousand spectators, who assembled to witness and applaud scenes of cruelty which one shrinks to think of. Our second visit to the Colosseum was by moonlight, when it looked grander than ever, in the strong lights and shadows ; and as we wandered through some of the dark passages by the light of torches, we almost expected to meet some of the shadowy forms of those who once filled those long, long vacated seats.

The immense size of the structure is better appreciated when one ascends to the very top, although it is difficult even then to believe (as has been computed) that "three hundred houses, twenty feet wide, and forty feet deep, with alleys between, could stand on the ground covered by the ruins of the great amphitheatre."

They are still making excavations in Rome, and disclosing wonderful antiquities which have been hidden from human eyes for centuries ; and we were astonished at many of the new discoveries in the Baths of Caracalla, and Palace of the Cæsars, both of which are vast heaps of irregular ruins. Arches, courts, columns half burned, and sometimes entire, meet the eye, covered with shrubs and flowers and grass—for nature seems to rejoice in making decay beautiful. Rooms with mosaic pavements have recently been revealed, the figures of the pavements retaining their forms and colors perfectly, while marble columns and statuary have been brought to light unbroken. We were very much amused with the jealous care with which the excavations are guarded. One of our party picked up a rough piece of porphyry from a heap of rubbish, as a little memento, and was immediately accosted by a soldier in uniform, who appeared so suddenly, that he seemed to rise up out of the ground. Trifling as the pillage was, it was necessary to place it again where it was found, and afterwards, wherever we went, we saw that as watchful eyes were upon us, as if we were expected to run off with the entire ruins.

It was rather refreshing to find something *not* in ruins, and we enjoyed very much our drive to the Borghese and Pamfili Doria villas, which are beautiful reminders of the old aristocratic life of Rome. Their present owners, however, are very glad to take the fees which are constantly brought by the throngs of visitors to these charming places. The grounds of the Villa Borghese are several miles in circumference, and beautifully diversified. There are avenues of grand old trees, and a profusion of fountains and ancient statues. The interior of the villa is rich in marbles, mosaics, statues and pictures, the most famous modern statue being that of Pauline

Borghese, the sister of Napoleon, represented as the Venus Victrix. She is reclining on a couch, and the position is most graceful, and her face very beautiful. It was for this statue that Pauline Bonaparte sat to Canova, with so little drapery about her, that a lady troubled with some scruples on the score of delicacy, asked her if the exposure was not excessively disagreeable. "Not at all," was the reply, "the room was thoroughly warmed."

Villa Pamfili Doria was once called Bel Respiro on account of its climate, and its charming variety of scenery. The drive through the grounds is very extensive and beautiful. They are laid out in gardens, terraces and plantations, with fantastic fountains and cascades. The views from many points are very fine and extensive, and it is an interesting fact that nearly twenty years ago, the republican troops of Garibaldi occupied these grounds, and for many weeks maintained their position against the whole power of the French army. Several distinguished men on both sides fell here, during the struggles between the contending armies. The villa itself is full of gems, and looked thoroughly comfortable and *inhabitable,* with its suites of charming rooms.

A touching memento met our eyes from one of the windows, in the shape of a cluster of dark green laurel bushes planted upon a sloping lawn, which were arranged in the form of letters, and spelt M-A-R-I-E, being *in memoriam.* The grass is kept closely cut, and the laurels trimmed, so that the letters are perfect in form, and the contrast of the dark green laurel with the light green turf, is beautiful.

On our drive home from this lovely spot, we saw two of the "Noble Guard" approaching on horseback, and knew that they were the forerunners of the Pope. So our carriage was driven up to the side of the street, and the masculine portion of its occupants alighted, and with hat in hand, awaited the arrival of his Holiness. It is expected that all in his way shall kneel, and we were surrounded by crowds who dropped upon the hard pavement with pious zeal; but he waved his hands as benignly over us, as over them. He may have suspected us of being heretics, and thought we needed his blessing all the more. His face is kind and benevolent, and on the principle that "the blessing of an old man can do one no harm," we were not sorry to receive the Papal Benediction.

We have not tried to *do* many of the churches, of which there are just as many as there are days in the year, but we have visited St. John Lateran, with its beautiful Corsini and Torlonia chapels. In the former is an exquisite picture in mosaic of Guido's portrait of St. Andrea Corsini, and in the vault beneath, a beautiful group by Bernini, representing the Virgin supporting the dead Christ. The expression of maternal sorrow is most touching and wonderful, while the holy serenity into which the face of our Lord has subsided after its hours of agony, is very affecting. It seemed a fitting illustration of the words of the blind preacher—"Socrates died like a philosopher, but Jesus Christ like a God."

Under a fine portico at one side of the Basilica, are the famous Scala Santa, said to have belonged to Pilate's house, and the identical stairs which Christ descended when he left the judgment-seat. There are twenty-eight steps, and they are ascended by penitents on their knees, who say a short prayer at every step, and reverently kiss every place marked by a cross, showing where our Saviour's blood has fallen. So constant has been this ascent during many years, that it has been necessary to cover the marble with boards, which are occasionally renewed. One can hardly believe that in this enlightened age such things are practised by all classes ; but richly dressed ladies and gentlemen are often seen side by side with the most squalid beggars—all crawling up together, and kissing the same ghastly crucifix at the top. It was here that grand old Martin Luther was toiling up on his knees, when the words "the just shall live by faith," came so suddenly into his mind ; and from that time his belief in the doctrine of justification by faith became so decided.

The Basilica of St. Paul, without the walls, is very magnificent, abounding in mosaics, porphyry, lapis lazuli and malachite. Four exquisite columns of alabaster support the canopy over the high altar, underneath which are said to lie the remains of St. Paul. The original church, which stood on this site many centuries, was burnt more than forty years ago, and princes and sovereigns have contributed to the erection of this gorgeous edifice.

In St. Pietro in Vincoli we saw the wonderful

colossal statue of Moses, by Michael Angelo, originally intended for the Basilica of St. Peters. It is very grand and noble, but does not seem placed in a position to show its remarkable power.

The church of the Capuccini contains the famous Archangel Michael, by Guido, called by some the Catholic Apollo, and said by Smollett to have "the airs of a French dancing-master." He is crushing Lucifer, his adversary, beneath his feet, and has, it cannot be denied, the look of "tripping on the light fantastic toe,"—but the figure is both beautiful and graceful, and the face full of sweetness and power. We went underneath the church to see the four vaulted chambers which constitute the cemetery of the convent, and contain the bones of many thousand monks; but when we saw the hideous array of bones and skulls which *decorate* the walls, and several skeletons standing erect, wearing the brown cloth robes of the order, we were glad to retreat as rapidly as possible. Everything is done to make these bones ornamental, but one cannot admire very much bouquets and garlands made of shoulder-blades and arms—neither does a lamp formed of a skull, and fastened to the ceiling by a chain of small bones, seem either desirable or elegant.

One day, in driving through the tomb-lined Appian way, we descended into the Catacombs of St. Sebastian, so long the hiding-places of the early persecuted Christians. It is impossible to visit these subterranean dwellings, without wondering how existence could have been borne there, even for a day; they are such extremely dismal, melancholy places, and the air so thoroughly chilling. Each of us carried a taper, which struggled for life in the heavy air, and only made the darkness more visible. We were conducted through long labyrinths, passage opening on passage, and now and then we entered small chapels with vaulted roofs. Everywhere there were sepulchres hollowed out of the soft rock, and the way was gloomy and dark. We all kept very near our guide, and I fully appreciated the thoughtfulness of a party who took the precaution to scatter small slips of paper from the entrance to the farthest point, that they might find their way back, in case the guide was seized with a fit of apoplexy! I do not remember ever to have rejoiced in the glorious sunlight more thoroughly, than when

THE CATACOMBS.

we emerged from those dreary abodes of the living and the dead.

The Protestant Cemetery is very pleasantly situated ; and were there no other graves there than those of Shelley and Keats, it would be an object of great interest. The solemn pyramidal tomb of Caius Cestius, seems to watch over the place, which is kept in beautiful order, and contains much precious dust, as many English and Americans are now lying there.

The "heart of hearts" of Shelley, which the fire on the shores of the Gulf of Spezzia could not consume, lies underneath a plain marble slab, in a lovely part of the grounds, while his friend, John Keats, is placed in an adjoining cemetery with the inscription he desired, engraved on his tombstone : "Here lies one whose name was writ in water."

> "'Tis writ, as thou hast said,
> Upon the cold, gray marble there,
> Each word of that wild, bitter prayer,
> On which thy spirit fled!
> But, oh, that injured name is known
> 'Far as the birds of fame have flown.'"

One could not but linger tenderly by the last resting-places of men of such loving, noble hearts, and brilliant intellects, whose brief lives terminated so sadly.

The Aurora of Guido, which Byron says,

> "alone
> Is worth a trip to Rome,"

is in a summer-house of the Rospigliosi Palace, and is approached through a garden fragrant with flowers. The picture is a fresco on the ceiling, and the coloring exquisitely soft and bright, while the radiant face of Apollo, and the eager steps and smiling faces of the graceful female figures representing the hours, are most charming. The beautiful horses, too, seem to exult in the scene, and plunge forward as if eager to drink in the glories of the new creation, while the flowers scattered by Aurora, look as if freshly plucked from the garden without. The picture is so attractive, that most fortunately, mirrors have been placed beneath it in such a position that we could see the reflection with untiring eyes, and without aching necks. The constant looking up we found so wearisome as to be at last unendurable.

Guido's famous portrait of Beatrice Cenci, in the Barbarini Palace, is familiar to every one through the copies which are scattered far and wide, and it was interesting beyond description to look upon the lovely original. The beautiful eyes, swollen with weeping, and the look of hopeless misery in the face, appeal so touchingly to one's sympathy, that they haunt one long afterwards. Then the loose drapery, the streaming hair, and negligence of dress, only add to the pathos of the picture, while the full *living* look of the eyes is almost startling at the first glance. All her grand heroism seems crushed out of her, and she looks now, when so near her execution, like a gentle, tender woman, needing the support and consolation which one would fain give, if it were possible.

At the Capitol, we were much impressed with the Dying Gladiator, so grand and proud in his mortal anguish. One feels like gazing in total and earnest silence upon such a death pang as rends his brow. It is a comforting reflection, in looking upon this most touching and tragical representation, that marble men cannot suffer, for although he

> "Consents to death, but conquers agony,"

it becomes at length painfully sad. It was a relief to turn away and look, in the same hall, upon the beautiful Antinous, so full of life and strength, and such a perfect model of youthful, graceful manhood. The Venus of the Capitol, too, claimed our attention, but I fear we did not appreciate her merits fully, for we felt very little enthusiasm for her cold, senseless beauty.

Our stay in Rome is so brief that we do not have many hours unoccupied of the first days of summer which greet us here. The weather is warm, but in no wise uncomfortable, and we are willing to spare ourselves unavailing regrets in the future, by seeing all that we can now, leaving to more favored ones the pleasure of a more thorough investigation.

> "Early in life, when hope seems prophecy,
> And strong desire can sometimes mould a fate,
> My dream was of thy shores, O Italy!"

Now, how many of its "unnumbered beauties" are becoming mine!

Naples, June 11.

Our last expedition in Rome was to the beautiful fountain of Trevi, where by the light of a full moon, we drank to our return. Ah, how glorious was that brilliant moonlit night, and how earnestly we hoped that this enchanted water might be a spell to bring us back, at some future time. *Nous verrons!*

Our journey here was through as beautiful a country as eye ever rested upon. Albano was to the left of us—on either side, there were mountains, with the valley between highly cultivated. The inhabitants live mostly in villages clustered upon the sides of the mountains, and for many miles before reaching Naples, the country is entirely occupied as vegetable gardens. About ten miles from the city we came in sight of Mount Vesuvius, with a cloud of smoke wreathing its top; and soon we were at the railway station, beset by a crowd of yelling Neapolitans, all eager to do something, or *get* something, for we have long ago discovered that beggary is one of the prominent features of Italy. Everywhere, we are surrounded by beggars; and they make their appearance in the most startling and repulsive manner and at the most unexpected times. On this occasion the little bright-eyed, dirty boys amused us very much, and it was difficult to resist their appeals for "maccaroni," made with such laughing faces, and frolicking somersets and gestures.

We were soon established in most sumptuous quarters, having nearly the whole Hotel Washington to ourselves—our rooms looking out upon the beautiful bay, with Vesuvius in full view from the windows, and lovely Capri in front of us. Our tea was served on a balcony overhanging the water, near a pretty garden, and it is difficult to imagine anything more thoroughly enchanting. In the evening we spent an hour at the Villa Reale, a pleasant promenade skirting the shore, planted with trees, and adorned with statuary. There was music, talking, walking, eating ices, and although but an ordinary occasion, it seemed quite like a fête. People in this delicious climate live out of doors, and make the most of everything in the way of pleasure.

Sunday was a national festival, and consequently, very unlike a day of quiet and rest. The parading of the military, martial-music, crowded streets, the national salute morning and evening, created a great deal of noise and confusion generally. We heard a very earnest sermon at the Scotch Church in the morning, or we should hardly have recognized the day as Sunday. In the evening, Vesuvius blazed up like a vast furnace, and we felt as we saw the various flashes, what vast reservoirs of fire and flame were within, and what havoc might be the result of their outpouring. There was also an

NAPLES.

illumination of the city, in honor of the festival, and many of the buildings looked very beautiful. The curious stalls at the sides of the streets, with oysters, and various unpalatable-looking eatables, were a great feature of the scene. The persons having charge of these delicacies were excessively dirty, and excessively noisy. We were not sorry to get out of the way of their importunities to buy, and hurried home, satisfied that an Italian crowd is an undesirable one to mingle with.

On Monday we drove through the Grotto of Pausilippo, above the entrance of which is the Tomb of Virgil. The grotto is about half a mile in length, and anything but inviting to eye or nose; being badly lighted, narrow and dirty. We found a charming country beyond, however, and followed the sea as far as Pozzuoli, where we were immediately attacked by ragged urchins, and filthy beggars, who surrounded and followed the carriage, offering their services as guides, and thrusting bits of stones, old coins, and dried sea horses in our faces. Annoying as it was, we could not but pity the poor wretches, and make some slight purchases. Everywhere we went, there seemed to be vagabonds waiting for their prey, and ready to dart out upon us, and we found it unsafe to admire a prètty child on her mother's lap, for we were immediately implored to give her something. "Datemi qualche cosa," is on every one's lips.

The ruins of a temple here dedicated to Jupiter Serapis, are very remarkable, although many of its beautiful columns and statues have been removed. The very stone, too, on which St. Paul landed, is shown, and we looked at it rather doubtingly, while we could not but pity any one, who either then, or now, had occasion to land in this vile, dirty place. But the drive along the shore was beautiful, and the country one of unequalled interest. We pursued our way to Baie, where Cicero, Horace, Pliny and Virgil once lived ; passing Lake Avernus and Lake Lucrine. Near the former Lake is the Sybil's Cave, immortalized by Virgil. Visitors enter it clinging to the back of an uncleanly guide, who carries a torch, and plunges through dirty water, two or three feet deep. When once within, they see "two small chambers, two bathing tubs, a flight of stone steps leading up to a closed door ; a few stucco figures very much begrimed with the smoke of torches, black walls, and blacker water!" Only one of our party was sufficiently classical to visit this charming spot, and we suspected that he was considerably disgusted, although, like all sight-seers who are taken in, he was unwilling to acknowledge it.

We preferred driving the fourteen miles from Naples to Pompeii instead of taking the cars, and passed through Portici, Annunziata, and Torre del Greco, all composed of long streets, swarming with people, carts and donkeys. The poor little oppressed, over-loaded donkeys, are a constant tax upon our sympathy. They are so brutally treated that I am often tempted to appeal to their hard-hearted masters for mercy, even with the probability of drawing down upon myself the sarcasm used under similar circumstances : "I did not know that my donkey had relations about here!"

On all sides during this drive, we discovered proofs of the devastating power of the volcano, while at the same time the soil is so fertile, that cultivation showed itself in the midst of the cinders and lava, everywhere to be seen. Pompeii itself, in all its lonely desolation, is very attractive, and one cannot visit it without inexpressible emotion. Yet, with a hot sun shining on the pavement, and not a tree to be seen, we found it extremely fatiguing to wander through its untenanted dwellings, and quiet streets. The houses are so small, that it is very evident the great enjoyment was in public life. The forum, the baths, the theatre, are all on a grand scale, and capable of accommodating great numbers. The ancient inhabitants undoubtedly lived mostly in the open air, as their descendants do. Their houses all have a central court, beautifully paved with mosaic, with a fountain in the centre. Around this, the family and guests could gather to gossip or rest. Some of these fountains were very beautiful, and adorned with statuary and mosaics. The rooms too, looking out upon the court, are often decorated with exquisite taste, the paintings upon the walls being wonderfully brilliant in color. The subjects are mostly mythological.

The streets are so narrow that one can almost jump across them, and there are ruts still visible, made by the wheels of carts. Now and then, high stepping stones are seen for the use of pedestrians, in crossing. Some of the houses must have been very extensive and luxurious—those of Diomed and Sallust were particularly so. In the wine cellar of the former were found the skeletons of eighteen adults and two children, who had fled there for refuge when the sudden calamity came upon them. The impressions of their bodies are still distinctly seen upon the walls, and one can imagine the agony and despair of these hopeless, helpless beings.

> "The palace is empty; the merchant's gold
> Is uncounted upon his floor;
> The affrighted bridegroom hath turned and fled,
> And the priest hath left his prayer unsaid,
> And the mourner stays not to bury his dead
> In that all-tremendous hour."

The Street of the Tombs in Pompeii is very much as it was originally, and the Tombs are nearly entire. Some of them are very beautiful, and they all show the reverence with which the ancients regarded the ashes of their ancestors. Intercourse with the dead was maintained by keeping their monuments and images in sight, and thus cheerfulness, not gloom, was associated with the idea of death. In a small museum, we saw the four bodies which have been found in recent excavations. Cinders had hardened around the bodies during their decay, thus forming a mould—liquid plaster was poured in, and thus the perfect forms obtained. One figure is that of a young woman, with her hand partly over her face, as if shutting out some fearful sight. There are two other women and a man thus strangely brought to the light of day, after so many centuries of darkness and decay. The museum contains some household remains and other relics, but the most valuable curiosities are in the extensive museum at Naples, where whole rooms are paved with mosaics brought from Pompeii, and decorated with frescoes, statues and bronzes, from the same source. There are also vases and jars containing figs, corn, and nuts, and whole loaves of bread still bearing the baker's mark. Rich jewels, too, are seen—rings, necklaces, head ornaments, armlets and anklets.

After our long walk we were glad to rest for a time in the museum at Pompeii, after which we sought refuge in a dirty little inn near by, where we enjoyed our luncheon with some very tame doves, which flocked about our feet picking up crumbs, and walked past us in the most friendly manner possible. Our drive to Castellamare and from thence to Sorrento, the same afternoon, was charming. The road, after leaving Castellamare, wound along the bank for miles, with a constant succession of varied views. On the right lay the radiant sea, deeply, beautifully blue, while the water at the base of the rocks beneath us assumed the colors of the emerald, or reflected other hues, according to the influence of light and shade, rock and depth. Capri and Ischia lying against the pale azure sky, looked in their vapory atmosphere like beautiful visions. On the left were shattered mountains, projecting crags, cultivated valleys—while orange, lemon and olive trees greeted us on every side. We passed from one scene of enchantment to another, until we reached the Tramontano Hotel at Sorrento, which we entered through a luxuriant garden filled with oranges, lemons, roses and myrtles. On the other side it overhangs a tall cliff, against which the waves are eternally dashing.

Seated in our pleasant rooms, their balconies high above the sea, with the balmy air, the glorious moonlight, the pure sky, and all the other bright surroundings, was like a dream of perfect bliss. The next morning was so fine, and the sea so smooth, that we were tempted to take a boat, with four stout oarsmen, for Capri and the Blue Grotto. The trip of twelve miles, we were told, could be accomplished in two hours, and our return much shortened, should the wind prove favorable. So we started early and gayly in a large, well-cushioned boat, with a striped awning—our neat-looking rowers beguiling the way with their pleasant Italian songs. The two hours soon passed, and we found ourselves near the rock-bound coast of Capri, while a small boat, looking at first like a mere speck, came dancing towards us, to bear us into the famous Blue Grotto. A hideous old man, and an equally hideous boy, took two of us at a time in the frail-looking bark, and after stooping very low, a wave sent us scratching through the small aperture which leads into the wonderful cavern, where the water that drips sparkling from the oars is intensely blue, and the lovely color prevails everywhere. The fascinating old man insisted on diving for our benefit, promising for five francs to come out of the water looking wondrously radiant. But we were more than satisfied with his present appearance, and declined, much to his disgust. Our sail home was short, and most agreeable, and after yielding to some temptations in the way of the beautiful Sorrento wood-work—looking upon the house in which the great Italian poet, Tasso, was born, and taking a short time for rest and refreshment, we left for Naples. Most reluctantly we left, for surely the wide earth does not contain a more lovely, bewitching spot than Sorrento.

With the sea caressing her feet, olive-clad hills protecting her on one side—flowers and fruits thrown profusely in her lap—balmy breezes, and bright skies her constant attendants—she sits in beauty, fairest of the fair.

We returned to Castellamare, by the same road over which we had driven before, and were not sorry to feed our eyes again on the same divine prospect.

Our pleasant rooms at the hotel, in Naples, looking upon Sorrento, which we had so recently left, seemed now to possess a new charm, as we gazed across the glorious bay upon what we might well call the "pride and darling of this delicious shore."

Milan.

The old proverb, "See Naples and then die," occurred to me, as we stepped on board one of the frail-looking Italian steamers at Naples, and were about trusting ourselves to the tender mercies of the treacherous Mediterranean. But the Cristofero Colombo proved worthy of its great namesake, and was both well-ordered and appointed; and although it danced the sailor's hornpipe, and floundered about generally more than was quite comfortable, we had a safe and tolerably pleasant voyage. The morning after leaving Naples found us passing the Island of Elba, and we all looked with interest upon a scene so associated with Napoleon's first exile. Nor did we forget that the last words of the noble, heroic Josephine were, "Isle of Elba—Napoleon."

We were not long in reaching Leghorn, and were much surprised to see a gang of Italian banditti collecting upon the deck, chained together in couples. They had been our fellow-passengers, and were on the point of landing to expiate their crimes—how or when, we could not learn. Some of them looked as if it might be mere child's play to cut off the ears or nose of a captive, as is frequently done by them, while others were quite crest-fallen. One of the party enjoyed the unenviable reputation of having committed several murders, while all were, more or less, desperadoes. As they went clanking over the sides of the vessel, strongly guarded, we were glad that we had never found ourselves

> "In an ill-starred hour
> Beset, and in a Bandit's power."

As we did not remember our former visit to Leghorn with much pleasure, we decided to remain quietly on the steamer, during our day in the harbor. We found it sufficiently amusing to watch the various crafts about us, and to hear the reports of those who trusted themselves with the brigands on shore. Another night at sea, and we were in Genoa, which seemed quite like home, as we went again to the Croix di Malta and received the welcome of the friendly landlord. Part of the day sufficed for us here, and late in the afternoon we entered one of the ten gates of Milan, and drove to the Hotel Cavour, pleasantly situated near a public garden. Our windows look out upon a square, in the centre of which is a beautiful monument to that great man, Count Cavour, to whom Italy owes so much.

It is pleasant to see the obligation to him so universally recognized, for in honoring him, Italy honors herself. This monument consists of a bronze statue standing on a marble pedestal, with no other inscription than CAVOUR, which a graceful female figure, representing Fame, has just written, and is still holding the pen upon the last letter.

Milan is so bright, clean and cheerful, and has such a decided look of prosperity about it, that we have enjoyed our sojourn here very much. The Cathedral cannot but astonish and delight with its wondrous beauty. The marble of which it is built has become mellowed by time, but is none the less effective because its dazzling whiteness has disappeared; while the thousands of statues of endless variety of sculpture, everywhere to be seen, render it most elaborately beautiful. The stained glass windows, some of which are very old, are very rich in coloring, and the pavement, composed of red, blue, and white mosaics, is extremely tasteful. Wherever one stands in this noble edifice, that particular portion forms a separate study, and the lofty arches and clusters of pillars render it most majestic and grand. We were present at one of the Corpus Christi ceremonies at twilight, when a long procession of priests with lighted torches passed through the different aisles, chanting their service. The effect was very picturesque, and seemed more like an act in some drama, than a real representation. In order fully to appreciate this most

MILAN CATHEDRAL.

magnificent structure, one must ascend to the roof, where its prodigality of adornments, forest of exquisitely carved pinnacles, each one surmounted by a statue, fill one with amazement. Our guide pointed a telescope to many very beautiful statues by Canova, which are nearly out of sight. The view from the roof is very fine on a clear day, comprising the plains of Lombardy, the Apennines, and the Alps, but we were not fortunate enough to see it in its perfection. The near view was very distinct, but mists veiled the mountains, and rendered them very obscure.

We were very glad to find a pretty little chapel in Milan erected for the use of Protestants. The service was delightful to us, and we heard a very impressive sermon on the Love of the Brethren as an indispensable characteristic of a true Christian. The congregation was not large, but we enjoyed with grateful hearts the privilege of again joining in our beautiful Liturgy with those whose language and belief were our own.

We went to the church of Santa Maria delle Grazia, in order to see in the refectory of the old convent, the famous Last Supper of Leonardi di Vinci. Engravings give one a very good idea of the picture, but the original has been so disfigured by time, neglect and dampness, and the colors are so faded, that it is difficult to form any idea of its former beauty. It is a remarkable fact that the head of Christ has been preserved more perfectly than any of the others, and the face retains much of its heavenly sweetness. Di Vinci was sixteen years painting this celebrated picture, and acknowledged himself unable to express his conceptions of the character of our Saviour. But his success has been considered far beyond that of any other artist who has attempted the same subject. It is a sad thought that in a few years the picture must entirely disappear—indeed, it is remarkable that it *now* exists, when one remembers that when Napoleon turned the monastery into barracks, this room was used as a stable, and that the picture was painted more than three centuries ago.

We have found the shops in Milan very attractive, and the beautiful new glass-covered arcade, so bright and cheerful, that there is a constant temptation to go there and sit by the tables in front of the Cafés, to enjoy our ices, and watch the passers by. The women look very handsome with their long black veils thrown carelessly over their heads, and worn in th place of a bonnet. Everywhere we see photographs of Prince Humbert and the Princess Marguerite, whose marriage has given so much satisfaction to their loving subjects. In all the jewellers' shops we notice ornaments of all kinds and descriptions made to resemble the pretty flower, the Marguerite. It has become the favorite decoration for both rich and poor, while the fair young bride herself is seldom seen without it.

Bellagio, Lake Como.

Our flight here was quite sudden, as one of our party was too ill to remain long, "in populous cities pent." So we took the cars for Como, the approach to which is exceedingly picturesque and mountainous. The town itself has lost much of its former importance, and looks like anything but the rival of Milan, which it once was. The situation, however, is lovely, and it boasts the ruins of an old castle of feudal times, which stands on a pinnacle overhanging the town. The scenery on the lake is beautiful in the extreme, and endless in its variety—so beautiful that it is impossible to imagine or describe its charms. The margin is studded with villas, while many of the hills are terraced, and myrtles, olive and fig trees give variety to the foliage. When we reached the Hotel Grand Bretagne on the border of the lake at Bellagio, we were thoroughly enchanted. It was delicious to sit by the shore and enjoy the glorious view, until a late hour in the evening. Our morning was spent on the top of the great cathedral at Milan—one of the most marvellous works of man. The evening was spent amidst God's great temples, whose towers and turrets are the mountains, and whose pinnacles pierce the skies; whose ceilings are the canopy of Heaven, lighted up by myriads of stars. How grand and sublime the thoughts inspired in such a sanctuary!

The next morning we wandered up a hill overhanging Bellagio, to visit the grounds of the Villa Serbelloni, which is on a promontory that divides the lake into two branches. The views in all directions are very fine, and the gardens embellished with every species of flowering shrub.

From various points, both branches of the lake can be seen, with the Alps in the distance, which looked rose-colored in the morning light. Late in the afternoon we took a small, gayly-painted boat, and were rowed over the lake to the Villa Carlotta, which is owned by the Prince of Saxe-Meinengen. We landed on marble steps which are built into the lake, and ascended two other flights, with vines covering the balustrades, and fountains at every landing-place that

> "gushed forth
> In the midst of roses."

One double flight of steps was completely covered with a luxuriant passion vine, which was one mass of flowers. We entered a magnificent vestibule, where are some beautiful bas reliefs of Thorwalsden, representing the triumph of Alexander. They were made for the arch at Milan, but afterwards bought for this lovely villa. There were many statues by Canova, among them the original plaster cast of his Magdalen. All the rooms contained pictures and statuary, and each window looked out upon more lovely pictures than those within. The grounds are exquisitely beautiful, with glorious views up and down the lake, and the whole scene was so like the one described by Claude Melnotte to his Pauline, that we could not but think he meant that very spot, although most other villas probably suggest the same oft-quoted lines,

"A palace lifting to eternal summer
 Its marble walls, from out a glossy bower
  Of coolest foliage, musical with birds,
  Whose songs should syllable thy name!"

To make this description still more like a charming reality, as we were walking through the enchanted bowers, a nightingale commenced pouring forth strain after strain of most joyous melody. We stood entranced for some time, listening to his delicious notes, which made the whole air vocal. As we floated back to our hotel with the glow of the setting sun upon the surrounding mountains, we felt that the half had not been told of this enchanting lake—doubly enchanting at this twilight hour.

Venice.

The next morning we had a three hours' row to Lecco, enjoying the exquisite views that met us at every step of the way, and then we took our last look at the lovely lake, and were soon on our way to Venice. The whole country seemed a succession of gardens, vineyards, and fields of grain, and Lago di Garda, with its beautiful surroundings, was in sight for some distance. This lake, which vies with Como in beauty, is nearly enclosed by the Alps, which form a mountain wall around it, and so soften its

VENICE.

climate that the most delicate grapes and fruits ripen upon its shores.

The approach to Venice was so sudden that we could hardly believe we were actually in the wonderful city which seems to belong neither to the sea nor to the land. Yet when we were seated in the funereal-looking gondola, with its black cushions and blacker covering, we felt how unlike the departure from any other railway station it was. As we glided along, we saw many evidences of former magnificence, in the palaces lining the canals, and soon approached one with a decided air of antique grandeur clinging to it. This proved to be our hotel, and it seemed odd enough to row up to the very vestibule, while a carpeted plank was thrust into the boat, on which we walked into the house. The ancient adornments, and evident look of fallen greatness were very striking in the various apartments, while the carved chairs and cabinets and chests, were enough to drive an antiquary wild. One could not but think of the fair Ginevra, and the "old oak chest" in which she had sprung

> "Fluttering with joy, the happiest of the happy,"

and which closed upon her forever.

Our hotel is but a short distance from the

noble square of St. Marks, where we can walk at our leisure, when we are tired of floating in a gondola, which we hire as we would a carriage elsewhere. In this warm, sunny weather, they are covered with a striped awning, sometimes in gay colors, which is a vast improvement on the sombre look which law has compelled the gondolas to wear.

We have floated under the Rialto, with its one beautiful stone arch, where formerly the princely merchants met to transact business. But its original greatness is gone, and the shops are small and mean and dirty. Undoubtedly Shylocks are to be found there still. We have floated, too, beneath the Bridge of Sighs, with "a palace and a prison on each hand," for we see the *outside* of things here, more than anything else, and gliding along in this quiet way, is a constant delight. Certainly, never was anything more remarkable than the canals of Venice—some broad, lined with magnificent old palaces; and others so narrow, with lofty houses on each side, that a ray of sunshine can seldom reach them—while the sound of wheels and horses' hoofs is unknown. We were rowed out to the Island of San Lazaro to see the convent founded by an Armenian who bought the island long ago for the benefit of his countrymen.

Lord Byron spent much time in study here, where pupils are educated for various professions. We were conducted about by a handsome young priest, in the long, flowing black robes of the order. He showed us the chapels, libraries, cloisters and printing-office—also the place in the library where Lord Byron studied; his portrait, with the turn-down collar, and his autograph in English and Armenian. The autograph of poor Maximilian and his broken-hearted Carlotta, were also there. In the refectory there is a small pulpit where one of the young monks reads aloud while the others are at their meals. A cruel custom which we felt had better be dispensed with, and a little pleasant, cheerful conversation allowed in its stead.

There is a fine garden attached to the convent, and a wonderful Artesian well, surmounted by a bronze cow and calf; and near by, some *real* cows, splendid looking creatures, whose milk is sold in Venice. We were quite charmed with everything, and felt that those were fortunate students who found a residence on that lovely island. Our return to Venice was by sunset, and we enjoyed the luxurious indolence which only a gondola can give—its soft cushions and gliding motion putting one into a delicious state of dreamy repose. In the evening we went to the square of St. Marks, where there is always music in fine weather, and where throngs assemble to enjoy it. All nations are represented in the various groups seated around the little tables, partaking of ices, and the scene is very gay and picturesque. In the midst of it all, the demands of the venders of small wares for the sale of their articles, is incessant. You are offered bracelets, nets and necklaces of shell work; shoes, slippers, and miniature gondolas, made of every conceivable material, and these things are persistently thrust upon you, wherever you may be.

It is difficult to believe there, that the splendor and wealth of Venice belong to the *past*, for the square itself is surrounded by objects still magnificent and perfect. The church of St. Mark, so rich and oriental in its magnificence, the palace of the Doges, the tall Campanile, the clock tower, the arcades with their gay shops and cafés, the old palaces, and the two granite columns—one surmounted by the winged lion of St. Mark, and the other by the statue of a saint—all form a picture of wonderful beauty; a picture so unlike anything else we have seen that we seem suddenly to have been transported to a different clime.

Every day at two o'clock pigeons are fed in the square, and these pigeons are so decidedly the protegés of the city, that any person found ill-treating them is arrested. It is believed by some, that they fly around the city three times every day in honor of the Trinity, and that their presence is a protection from an incursion of the sea. We saw them fed one day, and the moment the clock struck two, although scarcely any were seen a moment before, there was an immediate flutter of wings from all directions, and the pavement in front of the window from which the food was thrown was covered with a flock of the active little creatures. They all looked plump and well fed, and carried themselves as if quite conscious of their importance and safety.

The churches of Venice are among the finest in the world; and that of St. Mark, rich as it is in marbles and mosaics, is also rich in historical associations, being linked with the history of Venice for many centuries. In a chapel which is kept securely locked, we saw some of the treasures of St. Mark—among them a lock of the Virgin Mary's hair, the stones with which Stephen was stoned to death, a piece of the true cross, and a small scrap of the robe of Jesus. In the baptistry we were shown the altar-table, formed of a large granite slab, left in its natural state, brought from Mount Tabor, upon which our Saviour performed the miracle of the loaves and fishes. The stone on which John the Baptist was beheaded is also in the baptistry. In the church of Santa Maria Gloriosa di Frari, we found monuments to Titian and Canova—both of them beautiful and elaborate—the latter having been partially copied from a design by Canova himself, for the Archduchess Christine, at Vienna. The church of Santa Maria delle Salute, was erected as a grateful thanksgiving by the inhabitants of Venice, after the disappearance of the plague, more than two hundred years ago. It is beautifully situated on the grand canal, and contains some glorious pictures. Titian's Descent of the Holy Ghost, and St. Mark with four other Evangelists, impressed us very much. Tintoretto's Marriage of Cana, and some Madonnas of Sassofenato, are also there, and are very beautiful. We have wandered through the Doge's Palace

BRIDGE OF SIGHS.

with its Giant Stairs and great gorgeous halls and chambers, the ceilings of which are elaborately covered with pictures by Tintoretto, Titian, and Paul Veronese. From all this magnificence we descended into the dark dismal dungeons beneath, where in cells not more than six or seven feet square, with a few inches of grating, opening into a dingy gallery, the prisoners of state spent years of agony and despair. One could not but look at them with horror, and as we stood upon the Bridge of Sighs, with its grated windows looking out upon a narrow canal, we thought of the many who had passed over there, leaving all hope behind, and shuddered. We were glad to escape from these scenes of suffering, and enjoyed very much wandering over the Pisani Palace, belonging to an old aristocratic Venetian family. The long suite of rooms through which we passed looked so thoroughly comfortable, elegant and inhabitable, that it was charming to look upon them, and imagine pleasant family gatherings there. Many of the rooms were hung with rich satin damask, and the furniture covered with the same material, while handsome paintings, statuary, and various objects of value, decorated the room. In one bed-room we saw a superb counterpane of old Venetian lace over the blue satin covering of the bed. Some of the sofa pillows were also covered with this elegant lace, and we could not but think how much some fine ladies would have coveted this rare article thus lavishly thrown about.

Our last expedition in Venice was to the top of the Campanile, where we had a magnificent view of the Adriatic, the distant mountains, and Venice itself, securely seated on its seventy-two islands.

Verona, June 21.

We preferred spending Sunday in this quaint old town to remaining in Venice, which, with all its attractions, we found very warm. So we came here in a flash, by the cars, and drove into the old home of the Montâgues and Capulets, in a shower of rain which beat down upon us unmercifully. But we could see, even then, as we drove through streets of famous old palaces, and high houses with carved stone balconies, that it was a beautiful old town, and that its situation on the River Adige was most delightful.

After resting and refreshing ourselves at the Hotel, "Tower of London," the sun came out most gloriously, and we drove through curious old streets to the Amphitheatre, which is extremely imposing, and but little smaller than the Colosseum at Rome. In eleven hundred and eighty-four it was damaged by an earthquake, but is, notwithstanding, in wonderful preservation, and a most remarkable monument of the ancient Romans. Every one, when here, thinks of Juliet and her sad fate, and looks poetically upon the gloomy and dilapidated house of the Capulets, where poor Juliet talked to her lover from a balcony overlooking the garden. The house is now used as an inn for Vetturini—the court-yard is full of old carts and wine casks, and all the charms of the place seem to have departed with the "sweet saint" herself.

From the house, we drove to the tomb of Juliet, which we found at the end of a dreary garden, in a building looking much like a carpenter's shop. The custodian unlocked the door and we saw an open stone trough of rough Verona marble, with a stone pillow within it, and a hole at the foot for the admittance of air. It is a remarkable fact that it should be necessary to protect this monument carefully, in order that travellers may not carry it away, piecemeal. I am afraid our guide thought us decidedly incredulous, when we gave him his fee, and went half laughing and half scolding back through the mud to our carriage.

There are some beautiful churches in Verona. In that of St. Zenone, belonging to the twelfth century, there is a statue of St. Zeno, an African Bishop of Verona in three hundred and sixty-two, which is of jet black marble, and the effect is very strange. The church has some wonderful sculptures upon the bronze doors, and carvings in stone upon the front, which are very quaint and curious. Near the chapel of Santa Maria Antica in the heart of the city, are some most remarkable old tombs of the Scaliger family, which have stood in all their graceful beauty five hundred years. They are protected by a light iron railing, and the monuments are very high and very elaborate, the tallest one being surmounted by an equestrian statue. It has been said that these magnificent sepulchres are of such "grace and opulence, that unless a language be invented full of lance-headed characters, and Gothic vagaries of arch and finial, flower and fruit, bird and beast, they can never be described." So *I* shall not make the attempt. As there was no English service on Sunday, we went to the cathedral, where we heard very fine music, and feasted our eyes on Titian's Assumption of the Virgin—a sermon in itself.

Munich, June 25.

We left Verona at a very early hour on Monday, for Innsbruck, by rail. After spending weeks in a climate which we began to find somewhat exhausting, it was with a feeling of exultation that we found ourselves among the mountains, almost immediately after leaving Verona, and in the midst of the surpassingly grand and impressive scenery of the Tyrol.

The railroad over the Brenner Pass is a stupendous work, and is most creditable to those who projected and executed it. Were it not that it is so admirably managed, one could not but feel a sense of danger as the train, like a thing of life, winds its way around the mountains. The towering cliffs above, and the deep chasms beneath, inspire not only feelings of awe, but at times, terror. It was difficult, at first, to look out and see what was above and beneath, without a shudder; and had not our confidence in the care and skill of those who had charge been well assured, the expedition would have been almost painful. As it was, we all enjoyed the excitement, and when about thirty miles before reaching Innsbruck, we were greeted with a view of the snow-capped summits of the Tyrolese Alps, we could not find words enough to express our intense delight. We sprang from one side of the car to the other, unwilling to lose any of the glorious views that met our eyes, as we were whirled rapidly along.

Innsbruck is most charmingly situated on the River Inn, in the middle of a valley whose sides are formed by mountains covered with snow, and which seem so near that it has been said "the wolves prowling about the mountain-tops, look down into the streets." However, *we* saw no wolves, and soon after reaching there found ourselves at the most comfortable Hotel dé Autriche, situated in a wide street, lined with shops, many of which were beneath arcades, with dwellings above. Having ordered a carriage, a low vehicle containing two seats soon made its appearance, with a horse fastened by the head, and without traces, to one side of a huge tongue projecting from the centre of the wagon. We thought, at first, that the other animal had become disabled, and that one horse was expected to do double duty on this occasion, but we soon learned that this was the style Tyrolian. So we seated ourselves right merrily, and the horse started off at a brisk pace. But the way that playful animal managed to fly around in all directions, and still remained attached to the carriage, was most mysterious. Our drive was delightful, taking us by the triumphal arch erected in honor of the visit of Maria Theresa, and the golden roof over a bay window upon which one of the counts of Tyrol foolishly spent thirty thousand ducats in order to prove that his purse was not empty. We entered the Cathedral, in the centre of which is the splendid tomb of Maximilian I., consisting of a bronze figure of the Emperor in a kneeling posture upon a high marble sarcophagus, surrounded by twenty-eight immensely tall bronze figures, representing distinguished personages, male and female, mostly of the house of Austria. The whole effect is very imposing, but we looked with far greater interest upon the less pretentious monument of Andreas Hofer, who died a martyr to his devotion to Tyrol. The monument is surmounted by a fine statue of Hofer, dressed in his native costume, with his rifle slung on his shoulder, and an unfolded banner in one hand.

It is not strange that Napoleon should have feared the noble, brave, fearless spirit who could write, after being condemned to death by his cruel order, "It has been the divine will that I should exchange here in Mantua, temporary existence for eternal life; but God be thanked for his divine mercy, it appears as easy to me as if I were to be led out to something else."

It is pleasant to see so many of the pretty, picturesque costumes of the Tyrol still retained, and the men look very handsome in their embroidered waistcoats, and high-crowned, green felt hats, decorated with feathers. The women wear black felt hats, with a gold cord and tassel, and bodice waists. They all look sunburnt and brown from exposure in the fields, where they work with the men, yet they have a look of contentment; and we have nowhere seen so many wayside shrines, showing the devotional character of the people. Some of the figures of Christ on the cross are most revolting; yet these simple-minded people look upon them with reverence and awe, and never pass them without a prayer. When we were on the point of leaving our pleasant quarters at Innsbruck, our smiling landlord gave each of his lady guests, with his parting bow, a lovely collection of pressed Alpine flowers, tastefully arranged, "as a little souvenir," he said, a graceful courtesy which we all fully appreciated.

Our trip to Munich was very pleasant during the early part of the day, but it became uncomfortably warm in the afternoon, and when we reached Kuffstein, where our passports and luggage were to be examined, we longed for something better in which to rest than the dirty apartments at the railway station, which were filled with men smoking and drinking beer. We thoroughly realized at this place, that we were, indeed, in the land of beer, for the foaming glasses of this favorite Bavarian beverage greeted us on every side. Right glad were we when we reached Munich, and we found ourselves driving through the wide streets of a town which looked *new* enough not to be continental. And very new it is, in many respects, owing to the taste of King Ludwig, whose great desire it was to beautify as much as possible, and to imitate in his own capital, whatever pleased him in other lands.

Munich lies low on the river Iser, and is not picturesque or commanding in position, but is a very pleasant town, and wonderfully rich in works of art. Its public library is one of the largest in the world, and while in the Glyptothek and Pinacothek are seen most interesting statues and pictures by the old masters, there are modern painters and sculptors residing here whose works are unrivalled. We have found so much to enjoy here that we would gladly linger a long time ; but beautiful Tyrol has given us an irresistible longing for Switzerland, with its glorious mountains and fertile valleys. So we have rushed through the galleries, and looked hastily at the four exquisite peasant pictures by Murillo ; the one room glowing with Rubens' brilliant tints ; the gems of Wouvermans, Teniers, aud Vandyke. In the gallery of sculpture there are many valuable antiquities. The Barberini Faun, so called from the family to which it once belonged, is considered one of the most remarkable of its many wonders. It was discovered in a ditch of the Castle of St. Angelo, in Rome, and supposed to have been thrown down upon the Goths, who attacked the castle in 537. The figure is a colossal sleeping Satyr, reclining on a rock, and the look of perfect repose and deep slumber are most admirably expressed. The new Pinacothek contains many excellent works by modern painters, and we were particularly charmed with some of Verboeckhoven's landscapes, the animals in which seemed ready to walk out of the canvas, they were so life-like.

In the National Museum, we went through long suites of rooms, with elaborate frescoes on the walls, representing scenes in the history of Bavaria. There is a very rich collection of curiosities here, mostly of German origin, composed almost entirely of antique articles of various kinds—old silver, china, curious jewelry, quaint cabinets and chairs, and many other things long, long out of use. In the palaces of the king, we found much to interest us. The old palace which Gustavus Adolphus admired so much that he wished he could remove it to Stockholm on wheels, was finished more than two hundred years ago by Maximilian I. It is a curious specimen of the style of architecture of that day, and incloses four court-yards; in one of which is a handsome bronze fountain, ornamented with statues, representing Ceres, Juno, Vulcan, and Neptune, the four elements. The fountain was designed by the famous Peter Vischer of Nuremburg. We passed through long suites of rooms hung with faded damask and velvet, and family portraits, until we reached the luxurious apartments of Charles VII. One cabinet was hung with pictures in enamel, many of which were very beautiful. Napoleon once occupied these rooms, and in his bed-room are coverings and curtains of a bed worked with gold, which cost eight hundred thousand florins, and it is said forty persons were steadily employed fifteen years in embroidering them. In the new palace, which was finished only thirty years ago, many decorations and frescoes are after the style of Pompeii, and the floors are of various kinds of wood, exquisitely inlaid in patterns, each apartment differing from the others. The throne room, which is immense, contains twelve statues in gilt bronze, ten feet high, of the Princes of the House of Bavaria. These statues stand between columns of Corinthian marble, and all the decorations of the room are extremely rich, white and gold being the predominant colors. There are two rooms which are devoted to portraits of beautiful women who have lived, or still live, in Munich. They were painted by order of King Ludwig, and are thirty-six in number. Some are very beautiful, and Lola Montez, the most wonderful beauty of them all, once occupied a very prominent place among them, but has been removed by the present king. How strange her career! Followed by popular applause wherever she went, she was at one time at the summit of worldly prosperity. Her fascinations over the king of Bavaria were so great that he created her Baroness of Rosenthal, and Countess of Landsfelt—gave her large estates with feudal rights over a population of two thousand persons. A few years later, she was compelled to escape in the disguise of a peasant from Munich, and in a few years more died an humble penitent in New York. How touching these lines from her journal: "With what gratitude ought I to give thanks to Him who did not forsake me, even when walking in utter darkness and death. Oh, how long, long was He telling me that I should come to Him. I was indeed 'weary and heavy laden.' What has the world ever given to me? (and I have known all that the world has to give —*all.*) Nothing but shadows, leaving a wound on the heart, hard to heal—*a dark discontent.* Now I can more calmly look back on the stormy passages of my life, *an eventful life, indeed,* and see onward and upward, a haven of rest to the soul."

We have become somewhat initiated in the mysteries of bronze, at the great foundry which sends most remarkable specimens of skill all over the world. It was most interesting to trace the process from its commencement to the final completion, and we were glad to see many admirable figures which are one day to be in our own land ; among them a beautiful fountain with fifteen figures, which will be a delight to the citizens of Cincinnati, when finished. From the foundry we drove to the famous colossal statue of the Protectress of Bavaria, which is sixty-one feet high, and stands upon a pedestal twenty-eight feet high. She has a lion by her side, and in her right hand holds a sword for protection. Her left, which is raised, holds a chaplet to crown Merit. The figure is admirably proportioned, and it is difficult, at first, to realize its immense size ; but when one ascends it, and finds that the head will hold twelve persons, and furnish them seats besides, its vastness becomes very perceptible.

The Bavarian Hall of Fame stands on a slope a short distance back of the statue, and is a Doric portico composed of three sides, in which busts of many distinguished Bavarians have already been placed, and there are pedestals for many more.

We looked with much interest at the monument in St. Michael's Church to the memory of Eugene Beauharnois, Duke of Leuchtenburg, whose wife was a sister of the King of Bavaria. This son of the noble Empress Josephine stands in front of the closed door of the tomb, with his crown and arms lying at his feet. The attitude is simple, and full of dignity; his left hand is pressed upon his heart, and with his right he holds a laurel crown. Two genii, with sad and disconsolate faces, representing Love and Life, stand on one side, while the muse of History is seated on the other, inscribing the virtues and exploits of the hero. The monument is by Thorwalsden, and is very beautiful and expressive.

We have visited some of the studios, and have been delighted with many of the beautiful pictures which we found. Millnor's landscapes were superb, and it was pleasant to look upon Kaulbach, whose drawings are so marvellous, and to receive the cordial greeting which he always gives Americans. He was painting a lovely group of children for a favored countryman.

We had a delightful drive through the English garden, which is laid out with groves and shrubberies, pretty walks, graceful bridges and temples—a most charming spot. A branch of the Iser runs through the gárden, sometimes a strong but gentle stream, and then a torrent deep and rapid, foaming and leaping along, and making one realize that it is indeed the "Iser rolling rapidly," of the poet Campbell.

We made a short visit to the curious cemetery which is open to Protestants and Catholics alike, and looked for a few moments into the large room with glass doors and windows, in which, by law, bodies are placed immediately after death. It was touching to see the rich and poor lying side by side, and the efforts made to decorate them, and give a look of life, when life was gone forever. One beautiful little child was lying underneath an arbor of green vines, with a profusion of flowers scattered about her, and as she lay gracefully on her side, apparently asleep after her play, it was difficult to believe that those eyes would never open again. A string is placed in the hand of each silent sleeper, to which is attached a bell, which rings at the slightest motion. A wise precaution to prevent premature interment; and in one or two instances of suspended animation, the bell has been sounded. In case of an epidemic, when early interment is deemed necessary, a house of this kind must be invaluable; and it is strange that other cities do not consider it desirable to have such a safeguard. The grounds of the cemetery are prettily laid out, and well kept, and everything seemed to denote a desire to bring all the cheerfulness possible to this last resting-place of the loved and lost.

Zurich, June 28.

We are at last in Switzerland, having come to Zurich by way of Augsburg and Lake Constance. The first hundred miles of our way was through an exceedingly flat country; but as we approached Lindau it became more hilly, and everything assumed a Swiss appearance, perceptible in the houses and costumes of the people, as well as in the scenery. At Lindau, a strongly fortified town, we took a steamer on Lake Constance, and bade a final adieu to Bavaria, which was represented at the harbor by a monstrous stone lion in a sitting posture, with a not very amiable expression of countenance. We found the scenery on Lake Constance pretty and picturesque, but without wildness or grandeur. From Romanshorn, where we took the train, our journey was through a well-cultivated country, everything indicating a thrifty, prosperous people.

We drove to the Baur au Lac Hotel, and found it charmingly situated. The views of the green hills surrounding it, on which villages and villas sparkled in the sun, and the more distant snow-capped mountains, were very fine. In front of the house, a beautiful garden, cool and shady, borders on the lake. We felt that after the last fatiguing days, we had, indeed, found a haven of delicious rest. So we have quietly enjoyed the lovely lake, and have only ventured out, now and then, to take a peep about us. We looked into the heavy and massive, but plain and unadorned cathedral, in which the bold and fearless Zuingle denounced the errors of the Church of Rome. In the Arsenal we also saw the sword, helmet, and coat of mail, in which, when it was necessary, he could fight with other weapons than his tongue in defence of Protestantism. We also saw at the same place the cross-bow with which William Tell shot the apple from his son's head; but we looked at it with only a small amount of faith.

Zurich boasts of being the birth-place of many famous men, among them, Lavater the physiognomist, Pestalozzi, the teacher, and the two Gesners, one a celebrated naturalist, and the other a poet-painter. We have greatly enjoyed our little strolls about the curious old town, and they would have been still more enjoyable and comfortable, had the pavements been composed of anything but small, sharp-pointed stones. But there are few sidewalks, and we were obliged to hobble on as we best could. *Why* such stones were selected, we could not divine.

We have not in a long time passed so quiet a Sunday, and the pretty English Chapel was quite thronged with worshippers. The streets seemed deserted as we made our way to it, and it was with difficulty that we could find any one to direct us. Late in the afternoon we sat at the foot of the garden, enjoying the beauty of the scene—the lake so blue and sparkling, the shores richly wooded, and looking brilliantly green by the light of the setting sun. Suddenly, the snowy peaks of the Alps became tinged with a rosy light, which seemed to throw an illumination over the whole, and the effect was gloriously beautiful. We lingered until "'twas gone, and all was gray," feeling as if we had taken a peep into another world than ours.

Lucerne, June 30.

A delightful ride of two hours by railroad brought us here, passing through a beautiful country, and by the margin of Lake Zug. Our rooms at the Schweizerhof look out upon this loveliest of Swiss lakes, while Mount Pilatus rises high and imposing on one side, and the Righi, with its rich and grassy slopes, keeps watch on the other. We could not rest here long without a visit to the famous sculptured lion, dedicated to the memory of the officers and soldiers of the Swiss guards, about eight hundred in all, who were killed in defending the Tuilleries, and poor Louis XVI., and Marie Antoinette, in 1792. It is all the more remarkable as a work of art, from the fact that it is cut out of the face of a solid sandstone rock. The dying lion is represented lying in a grotto, a spear in his side, and his paw grasping the fleur de lis of France. It is wonderfully touching and impressive, and worthy the great genius of Thorwalsden, who designed it. One can scarcely believe, in looking at it, that it is twenty-eight feet long,

LUCERNE.

and eighteen feet high, yet such is the fact. The surroundings of the monument are extremely pretty, there being at the base of the rock a pool of pure water, creeping vines hanging from the top, while the pool is surrounded by maples, pines, and other forest trees.

We had a delightful expedition to Fluelen, at the head of Lake Lucerne, and were quite enchanted with the beautiful scenery. The lake is shaped somewhat like an irregular star, and as we proceeded, new scenes continually burst upon us. When we seemed to have reached an impassable barrier, a sudden turn, where the mountains and rocks came to the water's edge, would reveal some new picture of exquisite beauty, and wherever we turned, snow-capped mountains were visible. We looked with much interest at Tell's Chapel, erected on the spot where the gallant Swiss leaped from Gesler's boat when he was conveying him to prison. The Chapel is almost hidden by trees, and most romantically situated. On Sunday after Ascension-day, mass is performed there, a patriotic sermon preached, and the lake is gay with richly-decorated boats and flying banners. It is said to be eight hundred feet deep near the chapel. On reaching

Fluelen, we found the steamboat remained long enough to admit of our driving to Altorf, the scene of Tell's exploit with the apple. So we soon found ourselves looking about the curious old town, which is in the smallest and poorest canton of Switzerland, surrounded by grand mountains which towered high, high above us, and seemed to pierce the clouds. We found the colossal statue in plaster, erected in honor of William Tell, occupying the place from which the archer aimed at the apple on his son's head. About one hundred and fifty paces is the spot where the son stood, awaiting in agonizing suspense the arrow of his father—an arrow which brought about such great results. As we returned, Lucerne looked beautifully, rising gradually from the lake, its picturesque watch-towers, quaint old bridges, long walls enclosing the town, and Pilatus and Righi glowing in the evening sun.

"*Interlachen!* How peacefully by the margin of the swift rushing Aar thou liest on the broad lap of those romantic meadows, all overshadowed by the wide arms of giant trees! Only the round towers of thine ancient cloister rise above their summits; the round towers themselves but a child's playthings under the great church towers

TELL'S CHAPEL.

of the mountains. Close beside thee are lakes which the flowing band of the river ties together. Before thee opens the magnificent valley of Lauterbrunnen, where the cloud-hooded Monck and pale Virgin stand like St. Francis and his bride of snow; and around thee are fields, and orchards, and hamlets green, from which the church-bells answer each other at evening. The evening sun was setting when I first beheld thee. The sun of life will set ere I forget thee!"

How constantly has this beautiful description of Longfellow occurred to us during the last fortnight! At Lucerne we joined a party of dear friends, and our journey here by carriages was most charming. The first part of the way we passed by the margin of one of the arms of Lake Lucerne—then came Alpnach Lake, a little gem of beauty—then Lake Lungrn, and Lake Brienz, surrounded by lofty wooded mountains and rocks. Over the Brunig Pass, the scenery was very grand. Bald peaks and snow-clad pyramids formed a background—cascades leaped hundreds of feet from precipices, while the fertile valley of Meiringen, far, far below us, with the houses looking like mere dots in the distance, presented a picture of beauty not easily surpassed. From one carriage to the other we continually interchanged expressions of delight, and the words of the Psalmist constantly occurred to me: "*My cup runneth over.*" When we reached Interlachen we found ourselves quite exhausted, and were glad to rest at the Hotel Belvidere, which we have found all we can desire.

Directly before us lies the beautiful and majestic Jungfrau, more than twelve thousand feet high, covered with snow, while all about are other lofty mountains, their fresh green verdure, and rocky palisades contrasting most beautifully with the pure white garment of the lovely "young woman." Like a *very* modest damsel, she keeps her veil of mist over her face much of the time, so that when she chooses to lift it her beauty is all the more startling. When she stands forth glittering in the sunlight she seems almost unearthly in her dazzling brightness. Our stay at Interlachen has been diversified by various excursions, while the magnificent scenery by which it is surrounded, makes it a most desirable resting-place when we are disposed for quiet. The Fourth of July was, indeed, a day of rest and quiet, but we were somewhat startled in the evening to hear an explosion of fire-crackers on the lawn in front of the house. Some enthusiastic American had been unable to restrain his "gunpowder patriotism," and had thus given vent to his enthusiasm under the shadow of the Jungfrau.

The shops here are more tempting than we have found them at any other place in Switzerland. The display of wood-carvings is quite wonderful, and the onyx, amethyst, and crystal ornaments, really bewildering. One longs for a full purse, under such temptations as are set before us. We drove, one day, past the castle of Unspunnen, the reputed residence of Lord Byron's Manfred, through the beautiful valley of Lauterbrunnen, which derives its name, *nothing but fountains*, from the number of streamlets which precipitate themselves from the cliffs into the valley below. One of the highest waterfalls in Europe, the Staubbach, or dust stream, comes dancing down a height of more than eight hundred feet, and seems indeed "a heaven-born waterfall," for as one looks up at it, it appears to leap from the sky. The body of water is never very great, and by the time it reaches the bottom of the cliff it becomes spray, and is scattered by the breeze. When the sun falls full upon it,

"It veils the rock
In rainbow hues,"

and the effect is very beautiful. At Lauterbrunnen we took horses, and ascended the Murren by a bridle path, and the views the greater part of the way were most glorious—almost *fearfully* grand, at times. We were surrounded by an amphitheatre of snow-clad mountains and glaciers, and rugged precipices. The Eiger, the Monck, the Jungfrau, the Wetterhom, and other mountain peaks, all being in view—with eight or ten glaciers. During our ascent, we heard the roar, like thunder, of distant avalanches.

"All in a moment, crash on crash,
From precipice, to precipice,
An avalanche's ruins dash
Down to the nethermost abyss,
Invisible ; the ear alone
Pursues the uproar till it dies ;
Echo to echo, groan for groan
From deep to deep replies."

The noise is all the more startling from the intense silence which generally prevails in these high mountain regions, and one could not but think of the desolation and ruin such vast bodies of snow and ice might occasion should there be houses or villages in its course. At Murren we looked with sad interest at the spot near us on the mountain, where the lovely young English bride was struck by lightning a few years ago. A cross to her memory has been erected there since, and a memorial chapel in her English home, where her sad fate was so deeply and lovingly lamented. The descent of the mountain seemed so much more formidable than the going up, that we abandoned our horses and went scampering down on foot—a feat from which some of us did not soon recover, not being accustomed to such mountaineer exploits. The next day we went to Grindelwald, which is celebrated for the grand mountains surrounding it, and the two glaciers which descend directly into the valley, in the midst of vegetation. These glaciers are bordered by fir trees, which form a beautiful contrast to the frozen peaks of ice so near them. We entered a cavern cut into the glacier through the solid ice for many feet, and admired the exquisite blue of the cold material very much, but we found the atmosphere too chilly to remain long. Had we known that it was, even then, preparing to fall in, as it did, not long after, we should probably have retreated still more precipitately. At Grindelwald several of our party ascended the Faulhorn, from which some of the finest views in Switzerland are obtained, provided the weather is clear, which it seldom is. From the hasty journal of one of their number, I make a few extracts:

"All things being ready, we started off on our well-trained horses, and with our experienced and faithful guides, to make the ascent. It was a pleasant afternoon, and for two hours or more our path was through meadows and pastures, filled with an almost infinite variety of flowers of every hue and color. Nothing could be more beautiful. It was like a fairy-land, and kept us in a constant state of excitement. As we ascended higher and higher, the flowers began to disappear, and it was not long before we were in a region of perfect desolation—nothing but rocks and snow. We began to make free use of our shawls and overcoats, and yet we could not protect ourselves from the piercing cold. Our horses had to pick their way through the deep drifts of snow, as they could, and the dear, good creatures did behave splendidly. They were as careful as it was possible for a human being to be. Indeed, at times, when we were in despair, they seemed to feel their responsibility, and by dint of extraordinary efforts carried us safely through. At length, after some five or six hours of hard climbing, we reached the summit of the mountain, nearly nine thousand feet high!

"In all the valleys the sunlight had disappeared; but where we were, the sunshine continued for nearly an hour longer. Though bitterly cold, we stood, and gazed, and wondered, at the glorious views which presented themselves in every direction. We spent the night in a kind of house which has been erected there. I cannot say we had many luxuries, but we managed to get through the night comfortably. I found myself too high up in the world to sleep, and so amused myself by looking out of the window to see what the prospect was. In due time, the moon arose, and the mists having disappeared, there was a fine view of the mountains. At half-past three o'clock we were called to see the sun rise. And what a sight! Not a speck of cloud or mist rested on the mountains. By slow degrees the sun came up, and as its rays lighted up one peak after another, the beauty and splendor of the scene became indescribable. There we stood and gazed, in silent wonder, upon this marvellous display of the great Creator's power and glory. The whole Oberland range, as well as innumerable other peaks, were in full view. It was a sight for a life time. I could only exclaim, 'Glory, Glory Hallelujah.' Nobody who has not experienced it, can have the least idea of the feelings which such a sight awakens. I don't think any of us will ever forget that visit. I am sure I shall not. It seemed as though I was never so near God before.

"After breakfast we commenced our descent. Our guides led the horses, and we raced and chased each other over the snow at a great rate ; it was nearly as hard as the rocks themselves. In a few hours we were down again among the flowers and green grass, and were glad enough to get off all our extra clothing, for we found it very warm. The whole distance to the top of the Great Scheideck we had a full view of the mountains. There we took the usual route to the Reichenbach Falls, opposite Meiringen, feeling that we had seen what we never had conceived of, in the way of the awful grandeur and glory of mountain scenery. In some of the very narrow passes we found men with long wooden horns, called Alpine horns. These they would blow with all their might. The sound produced was loud and rather pleasant, but the echoes were truly beautiful. At first they were full and near, but by degrees they became fainter and fainter, and all the time receded, until they died away and were finally lost in the far-off distance. It seemed like something unearthly, and made one think of the notes of the celestial world. I was always glad to hear the sound of the Alpine horn. But sometimes, instead of a horn, these men would have a small cannon which they would fire off, making a most fearful and deafening roar. Immediately it seemed as though the mountains on both sides were filled with cannons, great and small, all blazing away at each other. From top to bottom, there was nothing but bang, whang, and roar! The effect of it all was, the ladies screeched, the dogs barked, the gentlemen laughed, the mules stuck up their ears, and the men politely asked for some money to pay them for their trouble. The people here are just like the people everywhere else ; whatever they do, they do for money, and the traveller had better always have his pocket full of change. When making our way out of one of these passes we became very much interested in the conduct of a little dog. He had been with us since we left Grindelwald, and every one had become very much attached to him; for he was a beautiful creature and as bright and lively as he could be.

"Our party was a large one, and strung along Indian file for a long distance. All of a sudden the dog became very nervous and went rushing about at a great rate. At one time, he dashed ahead, and then back he would come as hard as he could run. He seemed fearfully anxious, as though some great mischief were about to happen. We went on wondering what it all could mean, but soon the mystery was solved. We were approaching a place where they were accustomed to fire one of these cannons. The dog had been there before, and the noise of the cannon had scared him nearly out of his wits. True, he was a great deal more scared than hurt; yet like the rest of the world, he *thought* he was hurt, and that was enough. He remembered all about it and was exceedingly fidgety. But he behaved beautifully. Instead of running away, as we should have done, he didn't leave us for a moment. When we came to the cannon, for some reason it wasn't fired off; but the dog thought it would be, and he was unceasing in his efforts to hurry us past the place. He ran ahead, gave short, sharp barks, nipped the horse's heels, flew about the guides, and made a fuss generally. As soon as those in front were fairly by, he took the next, and so on to the last. I happened to be in the rear, and such an excitement as he was in, I never saw before. He did everything in his power to hasten me on. After some of his prodigious efforts, he would look me full in the face, as much as to say 'Old man, why don't you hurry? Don't you know there will soon be a great noise, and you will be hurt? *Do* come on.' Well, I did go on, and was soon past the cannon, and as the dog thought, out of all danger. Immediately, he became calm and trotted along in his usual way. I could not but think that this little dog had set us a noble example, and taught us a most useful lesson. If we should be as devoted to our friends, and every good work, as he was to us, how much good we should do!"

Geneva, July 20.

It dawned upon us one day that we could not remain in lovely Interlacken forever, so we took our last look at the peerless Jungfrau and went to Berne by way of beautiful Lake Thun, which is wild and picturesque part of the way, with views of distant snow-clad mountains, and near Thun, adorned with pretty villas and cheerful gardens. The ruins of an old castle with ivy covered walls, added not a little to the charm of the landscape.

We found Berne a most curious, quaint old place, very unlike anything else we have seen, and very pleasantly situated on the River Aar, which surrounds it on three sides. Most of the houses project over the sidewalks, forming an arcade in which are shops of various kinds. Everywhere one sees bears, either in wood, or stone, or iron, to commemorate the exploit of the founder of the town, who killed a huge bear which attacked him when he had commenced erecting the walls. Since then, the bear has been painted on their flags and stamped on their coins, and the town itself has been called Berne, which in the old German, means bear. Live bears are kept at the public expense in large pits surrounded by strong iron railings, and here crowds assemble to give them bread and fruit, and watch their gambols.

We were very much amused with two young bears which had all the antics of two playful kittens, without their grace ; tumbling about, standing erect, with their huge paws extended—climbing poles and falling on their backs with a force which seemed sufficient to crush them. Then rising and rushing into each other's arms again, and again tumbling over at full length. The whole scene was all the more ludicrous because the creatures had all the air of showing off for the pleasure of the spectators. The bridge over which we passed to the bears' den is a splendid structure of solid stone, with three immense arches. As we stood upon it, we discovered that one of the streets of the town was beneath us, and the bridge much higher than the tops of the houses.

We found much to interest us in the museum, which contains choice specimens of the natural productions of Switzerland in the way of birds, rare minerals, and stuffed animals. The hero among the latter, is the famous St. Gothard dog Barry, which is said to have saved the lives of forty human beings, by his sagacity and strength. He looked very life-like, standing with bottle and collar about his neck, as if about to start on his mission of mercy, and we felt that he deserved all the fame he has received. The cathedral at Berne was finished more than four hundred years ago, and is a fine Gothic building, with a curious carving over the principal door, representing the Last Judgment, with figures of the wise and foolish virgins on each side. The choir contains some curious stained-glass windows, in some of which are caricatures of the Romish priesthood. There are also richly carved stalls, heraldic emblems, and a monument to the founder of Berne, Berthold Von Zahringen. There are numerous fountains in Berne adorned with statues, and we found one in our rambles which was enough to strike terror in any juvenile heart. A huge Ogre is represented devouring a child, while several others are waiting their doom, stuck in his pocket and girdle. A troop of armed bears stands beneath, so that the escape of the little innocents is impossible. Altogether, the effect was decidedly impressive, and we wondered if the Bernese mammas were in the habit of teaching valuable lessons to their children by means of this monster.

Near the Ogre fountain stands the clock tower, where at three minutes before every hour a wooden cock crows twice and flaps his wings. A minute later a procession of bears walks around the seated figure of an old man with a beard, who turns an hour glass, and counts the hours by raising his sceptre and opening his mouth. In the mean time, a grotesque figure strikes the hour on a bell with a hammer, the bear at the right of the figure bows his head, and the cock finishes the performance with a third crow. All the figures are mere puppets, and the whole thing is very absurd, although displaying much skill. We visited with great interest the beautiful Federal Council Hall, a large building in palatial style, where the assembly hold their sessions. We were shown the different chambers and committee rooms, and were much delighted with the elegant simplicity prevailing everywhere. The debates are in the German, French and Italian languages, and often the discussions are quite as animated if not so stormy, as in our own House of Representatives. From the balcony in the rear of the building, we had a lovely view of Berne and its surroundings, the river Aar which flows at the bottom of a deep gully below, and the Bernese Alps in the distance.

After a night's rest in Berne, we made an early morning investigation of the curious booths which had sprung up in the night, in the principal street—it being market day—and we were

10

quite amused with the collection of articles, mostly for household purposes, thus brought together. The women in their white linen sleeves, embroidered bodices, silver chains and ornaments, looked very picturesque. An hour's ride in the cars brought us in sight of the ancient watch-towers, battlements and winding-walls of Freyburg, which is romantically situated on the river Saarine. The remarkable suspension bridges, one of them nearly three hundred feet above the rocky ravine below—the other at nearly the same height, and both almost a thousand feet in length, are objects of great beauty. They look so light, graceful and fragile, that at first it seems as if a breeze might blow them over ; but when one looks at the wires, and chains, and the rocks to which they are fastened, their wonderful strength becomes manifest. The views up and down the river, of the valley and the town itself, were beautiful as we walked over the bridges, which, hanging as they do in the air, trembled with the lightest weight. We remained in Freyburg a few hours in order to hear one of the finest organs in Europe, which at certain times in the day an organist is allowed to play upon for the gratification of travellers. Its tones are rich and full, and at times the music seemed almost unearthly in its delicious sweetness. When at last the imitation of a storm commenced, and the wind howled and the thunder rolled, seeming to shake the old church, which had stood for centuries, to its very foundations, we were all filled with silent awe, and sat breathless with amazement and wonder. The hour passed in that quaint old church of St. Nicholas, with its curious carved stalls, stone floors and most wonderful organ, will not soon be forgotten. With the notes still ringing in our ears, we left for Geneva, and just before reaching Lausanne, obtained our first glimpse of "clear, placid Leman" with its surrounding mountains, and pretty villages on the bank of the lake. These lovely views greeted us at intervals for many miles, and at length we found ourselves at a pleasant hotel close by the exquisitely blue waters of the Rhone at Geneva, our windows looking out upon Mount Blanc, the "monarch of mountains," in the distance.

We have found this beautifully situated town most attractive, and the drives in the neighborhood very pleasant. There are so many narrow shady lanes, hedges, grand old trees, and villas looking like English country houses, that we seemed almost to have been taken across the Channel again. We drove to Ferney, five miles from Geneva, which was for twenty years the residence of Voltaire. His chateau is beautifully situated, in full view of the lake and of Mont Blanc; and there is a long, lovely walk in the garden, formed by vines and trees growing over arches, so thickly covered, that the prospect can be seen only through gaps cut at regular intervals in the form of windows. In this secluded, and yet beautiful spot, Voltaire used to walk up and down, and dictate to his secretary. Two rooms in the chateau are left by the present proprietor as they were originally. They contain pictures, a couch, and a curious monument of earthenware, looking very much like a German stove, is placed on one side of the vestibule. The monument was designed to hold the heart of Voltaire, and bears this inscription: "Mes mânes sont consolés puisque mon coeur est au milieu de vous." At the entrance to the grounds there is a small dilapidated stone church with the original inscription, "Deo erexit Voltaire." The building looks now very much as if it were used as a place of deposit for hay and stubble.

Ferney improved very much during Voltaire's residence there. He collected industrious colonists, introduced useful manufactures, and was quite the "patriarch" of the town. He drove out every day in a gilt coach drawn by four horses, and was always addressed by the people as "Monseigneur." It has been said of him by a French author that "there is not, in the literature of any country, either in verse or in prose, an author who has written on so many opposite kinds of subjects, and has so constantly displayed a superiority in them all." How unfortunate that his influence was not always for the best! Voltaire used to say, in reference to this smallest canton in Switzerland, "When I shake my wig, I powder all the republic;" yet the whole world has felt the power of Geneva. From John Calvin the reformer, who hurled defiance at the Church of Rome, and denounced everything in the way of extravagance and dissipation, emanated the doctrines of our own Pilgrim Fathers. He may have been rigorous and severe, but he has made the whole world *think*. During his administration, John Knox was exiled from Great Britain, while "Bloody Mary" was on the throne, and resided in Geneva some years. What consultations these most remarkable men must have held together, and how little they suspected that remote posterity would feel their power!

The public library, founded by Calvin, contains over forty thousand volumes, and many valuable manuscripts and letters—among them a letter addressed by Calvin to Lady Jane Grey, while she was a prisoner in the Tower of London. There are forty-four volumes of his manuscript sermons, and twelve volumes of letters addressed to him. There are letters also of Jean Jaques Rousseau, which are quite different in their character. The situation of Geneva, at the southern extremity of Lake Geneva, and on both banks of the Rhone, is very beautiful; while the tall, handsome houses, of modern date, give a look of enterprise and thrift to the town. It is still divided into an upper and lower town, and the rank and condition of the inhabitants are perpetuated in these two divisions; the aristocracy residing in the upper town and occupying handsome mansions, while workmen and poorer shopkeepers remain in the lower town. It is rather amusing, however, that the industrial classes have the burgher aristocracy very much in their power, for in case of feuds, which sometimes occur, they bring their exalted neighbors to reason, by cutting off their supply of water—the hydraulic machine, which furnishes water to the upper town, being in their quarter. As there are over three thousand persons employed in the manufacture of watches alone, while other articles of ornamental jewelry require many more, the number of workmen is, of course, very large. It was quite a study to look upon the various and beautiful designs of the ornaments, and see the artistic skill displayed in their arrangement.

We never tire of walking upon the handsome long bridges which connect the two parts of the town, with the pretty Rousseau Island in the centre. The swans which swim gracefully about the island, are an attractive feature of the scene, while the intensely blue color of the waters of the swift rushing Rhone, is a constant theme of wonder and admiration. It is curious to see the hosts of washerwomen who occupy boats fastened to the bank of the river. These boats are about a hundred feet long, and extend for nearly a mile. They are generally filled with women, who stand side by side, rubbing the clothes with their strong arms, and keeping up a chatter which is quite deafening.

We made an excursion of a few days to Chamouny, from Geneva, and the drive there of ten hours was very delightful. We passed through several pleasant little towns, and the whole distance is diversified with the most interesting sights. Sometimes we were on the borders of the plunging Arve, beneath grand Alpine precipices—then there were frightful chasms, and beautiful waterfalls. One of these, called the Arpenaz, reminded us of the Staubbach, and is one of the highest waterfalls in Savoy. The stream is so small that it is broken into spray long before it reaches its first descent, yet it is extremely graceful, and after being nearly dispersed, it again collects, rushes across the road beneath a bridge, and flows into the Arve. The effect of the lost waterfall again assuming form, is very curious and beautiful. The rock of brown limestone from which it falls is very remarkable, its stratification forming a vast curve, which is very perceptible as the face of the rock is uncovered. It looks like an amphitheatre of mason work.

The valley becomes wider, after leaving the fall of Arpenaz, and some rich and fertile fields are seen at the base of lofty peaks, above the

CHAMOUNY.

village of St. Martin. We drove into a bustling inn-yard there, but could not rest until we had looked for the magnificent view of Mont Blanc from the graceful one-arched bridge over the Arve. The mountain, although twelve miles distant in a straight line, seems very near, the intervening space being annihilated by its vast dimensions. So we *were told,* for alas! for us, a sudden shower came on, and no mountain was visible to our longing eyes. So we consoled ourselves as we best could, with some of the delicious sponge cake and d'Asti wine, for which the inn is deservedly famous. Fortunately the storm was of short duration, and the rest of the way to the beautiful valley of Chamouny, we had views that were grand beyond all description, of the loftiest mountain in Europe, with its attendant throng of ridges of aiguilles, and glaciers filling the intervals. As this is a route much frequented by strangers, we found ourselves at all times and places beset by beggars, who made a speculation of their deformities, or insisted on selling mineral specimens, or dealt in echoes by firing a small cannon wherever its reverberations could be heard several times. It is not always agreeable to have one's view of a charming prospect intercepted by a goitre, and we considered these poor wretches a great nuisance. Late in the afternoon, we found ourselves beneath the shadow of Mont Blanc, and a glorious sunset illuminating the whole range, left us nothing to desire.

The next morning we walked upon the "Mer de Glace," which fully realized the beautiful description of Coleridge, and seemed, indeed, like

"torrents that heard a mighty voice
And stopped at once, amid their maddest plunge."

The beautiful blue color of the ice, and its great purity, can only be seen by looking down into the crevices, which are so frightfully deep that one cannot but shudder at the thought of a misstep in climbing over their icy billows.

It is said that an Alpine hunter, some years ago, in passing over the Mer de Glace, lost his hold and slipped into one of these fearful crevices. By catching himself in his swift descent against the points of rocks and projecting ice, his fall was so broken that he reached the bottom alive. But what a prison was he in! On either hand, the icy walls rose up to heaven, above which he saw only a strip of blue sky. A little stream of water at his feet, formed by the slowly melting glacier, suggested to him the idea that in following it, he might find some outlet. He picked his way, in terror, down, down the mountain side, till his course was stopped by an immense cliff that rose up before him, while the river rolled darkly below. There was no time for delay. Death was before him in either case, and pausing only an instant, he plunged into the stream. One minute of breathless suspense—a sense of darkness, coldness, and swift gliding motion, and then a light began to glimmer on the waters. The next instant he was amid the green fields, and the flowers, and the summer sunshine of the Vale of Chamouny. As we looked at the source of the Arveiron, rushing from beneath a lofty arch of ice at the foot of this glacier, we could not but think of this fortunate escape—so different from the fate of most Alpine climbers who have the misfortune to make a false step in slippery places.

The scenery where the Arveiron begins to "rave ceaselessly" is very grand. The deep blackness of the vault of ice contrasted with the beautiful blue where the light is transmitted through the ice, is very striking. Enormous rocks are piled up which have been brought down by the glacier from the mountains above, and are deposited in the bed of the river. Sometimes it is very dangerous to venture too near, lest one should be crushed by the falling stones. Yet every year there are accidents resulting from careless exposure of life, and a too eager desire to penetrate forbidden places. The foolhardiness seems all the more strange, when there is so much to be *safely* seen, which will give one memories that will be a life-long delight.

Vevay, July 31.

We have spent nearly a fortnight in this picturesque spot, with its swelling hills and vine-clad slopes in the background, and beautiful Lake Leman with its snow-crowned mountains lying before us. The Grand Hotel, so thoroughly comfortable and elegant, has been indeed a "haven of rest" to us, and the quiet days passed here, looking out upon most beautiful, and at the same time most sublime scenes, cannot soon be forgotten.

Our enjoyment of the "holy quiet of Nature" has been perfect, and day after day have we sat by the lake shore, drinking in the exquisite beauty of the scene. We were shocked and saddened one day, however, when we saw a sail-boat capsize just before us, in which was a young Greek gentleman, who had won all hearts by his kindly manners, and who had just parted with his friends, in gay spirits, for a short sail upon the lake. Before help could be obtained, he sank, and we were forcibly reminded that "in the midst of life, we are in death." It seemed the work of *seconds* only, and the groups gathered upon the lawn, grew silent and sad, and only spoke in whispers, where so short a time before, all was gayety and merriment. Our hearts ached for the mother in her far away Greek home, who thus lost her only child, and whose husband some years before had been drowned in the Adriatic.

One pleasant day we took the steamer to Villeneuve, at the head of the lake, and on our return stopped at the renowned castle of Chillon, which stands firmly upon an isolated rock within a stone's throw of the shore, and yet is surrounded by deep water. It is approached by a wooden bridge, which is firm now, but was formerly a drawbridge, thus making the castle inaccessible. Its gray walls have stood firmly more than six hundred years, and during that time, what scenes have been transacted within these walls! Its crypts once served as a place of confinement for persecuted Christians, and afterwards for prisoners of state. On a block of marble in one of the dungeons, tradition says two thousand Jews were beheaded, partly on account of their religion, and that the nobles might secure their gold. Near this place is a deep arch in the wall which once contained an image of the Virgin, before which the condemned were allowed to pray before they were hung upon a huge beam near by. Then there was the *Chambre des Oubliettes*, where in lawless times, prisoners of state were dragged without trial, and made to kneel upon a trap door, before the image which Catholics so much revere and love. While thus asking for mercy, the trap door fell at a given signal, and the poor wretch was dashed in pieces, far, far below. One could not but shrink and shudder in looking into the fearful abyss. But the place of deepest interest was the dungeon in which the Swiss patriot Bonnivard was kept for six years chained to one of the low pillars which support the roof—one of the "seven columns massy and gray" of which Lord Byron speaks, and in which he has inscribed his name in large letters. Several of the columns have iron rings in them, and near the one to which Bonnivard was fastened, and where the length of the chain only allowed him to walk a few feet,

> "'twas trod
> Until his very steps have left a trace
> Worn, as if the cold pavement were a sod."

The dungeon is on a level with the lake, and the rippling of the water is distinctly heard, while through the narrow loop-holes which admitted the light, we could see

> "the small green isle
> Which in his very face did smile,"

with its three tall trees. After the Genevese were released from the Savoyard yoke, the castle was besieged by seven thousand Bernese, and the prison doors opened. The words "Bonnivard, thou art free," must have sounded like music in ears so long unaccustomed to any voice but that of his jailor. Those six years had made Geneva protestant and independent, and Bonnivard was rewarded for his years of misery and suffering, in the affection and trust bestowed upon him during the rest of his life. In sixteen hundred and forty-three, a little more than one hundred years after this event, there was inscribed over the governor's entrance, the words, "May God bless all who come in and go out." A pious wish, which a few centuries before would hardly have been allowed. But as the castle is now used only as a magazine for military stores, its scenes of cruelty are over.

The state chambers of the Duke and Duchess of Savoy were shown us, and were very curious specimens of the taste of those times. The wooden ceilings are very much carved, and there are some attempts at ornament upon the walls and windows. A very large audience-chamber, with an immense fireplace, has the various coats of arms of different Swiss cantons painted upon the wall; each governor, while the Bernese had control, having added his own arms, name and inscription. It was pleasant to see that *all* had not been desolation and misery within these walls, and as we approached the bridge to leave, we were most happy to accept the invitation of an old soldier into his tidy apartment which he seemed proud to show us, while he enlarged upon his comfort as custodian there. Chillon, with its round towers, massive walls, moat and drawbridge, and charming situation, is a most picturesque and beautiful specimen of one of the castles of feudal times. As we walked slowly away, we turned again and again to gaze upon a scene so full of beauty and interest.

In the church of St. Martin's at Vevay, which is beautifully situated in the midst of trees and vineyards, the remains of the regicides Ludlow and Broughton are buried. The latter read the sentence of death to Charles I., and both died in exile. As we looked at the lovely prospect from the eminence on which the church stands, our thoughts wandered across the ocean to the New England town where we had so often stood by the graves of Whalley and Goffe, who were also exiled at the same time and endured such privations in our own land. We could not but feel that they were more fortunate who sought a home by the borders of Lake Leman.

Basle, August 3.

We are now on the brink of the Rhine, which rushes past our hotel with great force and power, and is here a magnificent stream. We were welcomed to our "Hotel des Trois Rois" by the gilded effigies which decorate the front, and have found Basle a clean, thriving town, full of handsome residences and pleasant streets. The Cathedral is a curious edifice placed in a commanding situation, and painted red. It is decorated with quaint carvings and statues—among them St. George and the Dragon are very prominent. On one side of the church are extensive and picturesque cloisters, which are a succession of halls and open spaces, and still serve for burial places, as they have done for centuries. Many reformers are buried here, and as the cloisters extend to the verge of the hill overlooking the river, it is supposed to have been the favorite resort of Erasmus, who died here in fifteen hundred and thirty-six, and whose tombstone is in the cathedral. Basle has acquired a high reputation in the religious, literary and artistic world; for while it has been regarded as the stronghold of Methodism in Switzerland, its University is very flourishing, and the collection of paintings by Holbein in the Museum are evidences of the power of the great master who made this town his home. We were much interested in our visit to the Mission House, the object of which is to educate missionaries for the promulgation of the Gospel among the heathen. Every facility is given to the student to acquire the desired knowledge, and we found the Museum full of curiosities which had been sent from various lands by those who had been educated there, and were now laboring for their Master in the missionary field. Just forty years ago, the society of Basle projected their mission to Africa, and sent four missionaries to Akropong. Now, that community, including converted natives, consists of more than ten thousand members. The children of missionaries are kindly cared for, and educated by the society at Basle, and we saw more than one hundred and fifty of these little creatures playing about the grounds of the institution, looking well and happy. It seemed strange enough to find upon the wall at the head of one little bed, the photographs of faces well known to us, and to learn that the little son of an American missionary to Africa was enjoying the benefits of this pleasant home, his father having been sent under the auspices of the Basle society.

The laws formerly were very strict with reference to Sunday, but they have been much modified. All are not compelled to dress in black to go to church, as was once the law, and every variety of costume is seen. The enormous bow of black ribbon which the peasant women wear on the top of their heads looks very strange, but is not ungraceful, although, as a means of protection to the face, it amounts to very little.

Strasburg.

The beautiful open-work spire of the noble cathedral announced our approach to this town long before we could see anything else, and it seemed to penetrate the very clouds. A nearer view did not dispel the illusion, we found, and when we remembered that the spire, so delicate and elaborate in its workmanship, was finished more than fifty years before America was discovered, we could not but wonder at the skill which had made the light, airy, graceful structure so durable. The interior too, with its rich sculptures and gorgeous stained glass, is very beautiful, the circular window being forty-eight feet across, and exquisite in coloring. The famous clock, which is a marvel of skill, and was invented three hundred years ago, attracts strangers always, and we were fortunate in being in the cathedral at the hour of twelve, when the images and puppets were set in motion, and the cock gave its triumphant crow. Besides this, the clock calculates eclipses, teaches the sun and moon their courses, and does many other things, equally wise and learned.

From the cathedral, we drove to the church of St. Thomas, which contains the monument to

STRASBURG CLOCK.

Marshal Saxe, erected to his memory by Louis XV. The figure of the hero himself, represented as calmly descending into his grave, is very noble, and a very beautiful female figure, representing France, who is endeavoring to detain him, and stay the approach of death, is most touching in its tenderness of expression. There are, in the same church, some curious relics of the past, in the shape of two bodies, said to be those of the Count of Nassau and his daughter, who died more than a century ago. They are kept in glass coffins, and are in a wonderful state of preservation, although by no means *beautiful.* The gay brocade silk dress, and wreath of faded artificial flowers, on the poor shrunken head of the young lady, seemed a mockery; and the spectacle was rather disgusting, although very curious as representing the costume of that day.

Our visit to the establishment for the training of deaconesses was very interesting, and we found everything in beautiful order, and the sisterhood apparently very happy in the works of mercy and charity to which they consecrate themselves. The institution was founded twenty-six years ago, and during that time, thousands have received their tender care and ministration, which they bestow without reward—and as their report says, "to prove their gratitude to Him who has saved them."

The town is full of nice shops, and but for the vile odors which saluted us everywhere we went, we should have enjoyed peeping into them ; but the pleasure of walking about the streets was much lessened by the sufferings to which one's nasal organs were exposed. So we retreated to our hotel, and being in the region

> "Where the ducks fly about with the true pheasant taint,
> And the geese are all born with the liver complaint,"

we of course tasted a "pate de foie gras," for which the place is so famous ; and as there are thirty-eight large breweries worked by steam in the town, we also had most excellent opportunities of indulging in an unlimited amount of beer. The inducements to partake of that beverage were certainly very great, from the fact that a tavern near by bore the following inscription ; "Strong beer and wine of the first quality. Customers drinking more than twelve glasses, will be sent home in a cab, free of charge, in case they are unable to walk."

Baden-Baden, August 4.

We are now in this fashionable German watering-place, so charmingly situated among the hills forming the Black Forest range. The valley here is very narrow, and the town with its fine trees, shrubbery, and pretty gardens, is all one pleasure ground. Indeed *pleasure* seems the main end and object of life here, for one encounters very few invalids, and all is elegance and display. Princes, blacklegs, and gayly-dressed ladies are equally numerous, and the place is adapted to all tastes. There are balls, concerts, and gaming-tables, for those who like them, and for those who prefer quiet, there are shady walks, dark woods, and deep valleys, where the solitude is complete. There are thirteen springs in the town, all of which are hot, and the temperature never varies at any season of the year. It is used mostly for bathing, but a few invalids resort to the handsome temple which serves as pump-room, and drink the waters very early in the morning. We found one trial of its qualities quite enough.

The Kursaal, which is the celebrated gambling establishment, is the great point of attraction here. The whole edifice is splendid in gilding, upholstery, and immense chandeliers. It offers all its accommodations to visitors, free of charge, and throughout the season there is a concert of instrumental music every evening. There are free reading-rooms, attractive refreshment-rooms, and a magnificent room for concerts and balls. Here are the roulette tables, at which two persons preside with great solemnity, to mark the game, while groups of anxious gamblers are seated around—men and women, old and young. It was painful to watch the eagerness of some of the players, although there was less excitement than we were prepared to expect, and everything was done quietly and silently. As those who stake the money have really nothing to do with the process by means of which it changes hands, it is, of course, all sheer chance. Yet, stupid as it is, people sit there by the hour, losing at one moment, and winning at the next, until they have perhaps lost everything, or have won all they desire, for the present. So it goes on, day after day—so it has done for many years, and despair, ruin and suicide, have been the results very often. Fortunately the players do not play against each other, but against the *bank*, so that there are less quarrels than there would be, if it were more like private gambling. Still, the misery caused here has been immense, and it is a blessed thing that it is all to be done away with before long, by order of the Prussian government.

We took a delightful drive of two miles through an avenue of shady oaks to Lichtenthal, which is pleasantly situated near a beautiful valley, and afterwards ascended the hill above the town, on the summit of which are the picturesque ruins of the old castle. It was the earliest residence of the ancestors of the house of Baden, and so situated as to afford complete security from the attacks of foes. From the galleries around its battlements, the views are very extensive and beautiful, comprising the Black Forest, with its dense woods, enclosing verdant valleys—the town of Baden at your feet—villages, convents and church spires in the distance, while on the other side, the path of the Rhine may be traced far away. All this, seen in the light of the setting sun, made a picture long to be remembered.

Heidelberg.

We came in sight of the most magnificent ruin in Continental Europe, in a little more than three hours from Baden; and as the castle is on the brow of a high hill which towers directly behind the city, it is almost constantly in view.

It is, indeed, one of the wonders of the world, for while it has been repeatedly captured and dismantled, twice struck by lightning, and in sixteen hundred and eighty-nine blown up by the French, it still stands gloriously beautiful in its decay. The walls, in some parts, are seventeen feet thick, and the cunning hand of Art was busy for many centuries, raising and adorning them. Over the windows and doorways and chimneys, are exquisite sculptures, while the outer walls are richly ornamented with statues. Many of them are entire and beautiful, but others have been sadly maimed, and present a very grotesque appearance, with noses sliced off, and arms and legs wanting.

The most magnificent portions of the castle were built for the English Princess Elizabeth, daughter of James I. and granddaughter of Mary Queen of Scots, the wife of the Elector, Frederic V., afterwards king of Bohemia. Her married life commenced most brilliantly here, and one cannot but look sadly upon the beautiful palace, garden terrace and triumphal arch, erected in her honor, when one thinks of the misery of her later years. But she *would* be a queen, and when her husband hesitated to accept the crown of Bohemia, she exclaimed: "Let me rather eat dry bread at a king's table, than feast at the board of an Elector!" So her desire was fulfilled, more literally than she wished or expected, for she and her children lived to eat dry bread, and were dependent on charity for the necessaries of life.

There is an endless variety to the ruins of the castle, and the architecture of different ages strikes the eye in wandering about. There are towers, large and small, fantastic gables, a moat and drawbridge, and a curious old chapel. The ruins are all the more impressive from the ivy which covers them—the large stalks of which show its great age; while in many parts large trees are growing from the top of the walls. The Rent Tower, which was blown up by the French, but was too strongly built to be demolished, has a grove of linden trees on its summit. The Heidelberg Tun, which holds nearly three hundred thousand bottles of wine, is among the curiosities of the castle, and the funny image of the old man that used to keep it, is shown in the same cellar. The Tun is shaped like a hogshead laid lengthwise, and over the top is a floor, where in former times, when it was filled, it was customary to dance around the bunghole. It has remained empty a hundred years, however, so that the voice of merriment has long ceased in that cellar, although the Tun is kept in repair.

The view from the garden terrace is beautiful and extensive, comprising the romantic town crowded in between the mountain and the rushing stream of the Neckar, which is seen, for a long distance, winding through fertile vales. The spot where the students fight their absurd duels, on the opposite side of the river, was pointed out to us, and we afterwards met many of these youths, with their faces gashed and scarred and plastered up. They wear little caps of different colors, about as large as a saucer, and much that shape, to denote the corps, or societies, of which they are members, and are frequently accompanied by an immense dog. Their duels are seldom dangerous to life or limb, and the aim is always to disfigure the face by sword cuts, and not to injure seriously. As there are generally about seven hundred students in Heidelberg, these cuttings and slashings are very common, and one scarcely stirs out without meeting some one who is enjoying a fresh wound. Heidelberg does not contain very much to interest transient visitors, but the church which has been for centuries occupied by Romanists and Protestants, is very curious—a thick partition wall running between the nave and the choir, the former belonging to the Lutherans, the latter to the Catholics. There is also a most elaborately carved stone house, black with age, very quaint in its appearance, which was erected in fifteen hundred and ninety-two, by a French Protestant who narrowly escaped the massacre of St. Bartholomew. His gratitude is expressed in several devout inscriptions in Latin on various parts of the building.

We drove out to the Wolfs Brunnen, so named from a spring which rises there, and from a tradition that Jetta, an enchantress, who resided there, was torn to pieces by a wolf. The place is famous for its trout, which are kept in a pool, and fed with other fish caught in the river. It is a great place of resort, but we were by no means fascinated with its attractions, for it seemed damp, dark and gloomy, while the dead fish floating on the top of the pool gave us a distaste for the gorged trout beneath the water, on which parties come there to dine. We found the Swiss Cottage far above, on the mountain, much more attractive, with its beautiful views up and down the valley, and the wonderful castle beneath us, its red ivy-covered walls gleaming in the setting sun.

Frankfort.

Our stay in this pleasant town, with its numerous white houses, so different from most continental cities, has been very brief, but we have driven through its broad, cheerful streets, and into the narrow dark lanes of the Jews' quarter, where the curious wooden buildings have gables overhanging their basement stories, out of the windows of which opposite neighbors might almost shake hands. In this odd place, the famous Rothschild family lived for many years, and here the venerable mother preferred remaining all her life, when she might have occupied a palace near by.

We have thoroughly enjoyed the great art glory of Frankfort, the Ariadne of Dannecker, of which it has been said that "travellers on the road to Italy praise it, and all on their way home criticise it." The ease and grace of the attitude, the position of the head, and the exquisite beauty of the form are most charming, and it seemed to us faultless. One could not but think of the poor little boy whose scrawls with chalk and charcoal, on the marble of the stonecutter who lived next door to him, were the occasion of constant beatings from his father. But blows and lockings-up could not quench the genius of Dannecker. Neither could poverty and loneliness, home-sickness and heart-sickness among the ruins and relics of Rome. When very old, after receiving all worldly honors, Canova paid him a visit, and was so struck by his child-like simplicty, pure, unworldly nature, genuine goodness and happy temperament, that he called him "The Blessed."

Hamburg.

We are again in the midst of the gayety and gambling of a much frequented watering-place. The Kursaal, with its pleasure-grounds and music, is very attractive, while the virtues of the medicinal springs attract many who need the benefit of their healing waters. One difference between this place and Baden-Baden seems to be, that here gambling goes on through the entire year, except Sundays, and fête days, making three thousand six hundred play-hours in a year. It is impossible to imagine the amount won and lost during that time. Disgusted as we were with gambling, we found ourselves watching the games with interest; and we saw one young man win a large pile of gold, and by degrees lose every particle of it; when he left the table with a countenance perfectly unmoved, although his eagerness to win had been almost painful. One of the markers of the game, a solemn-looking individual, kept uttering the words, "Le jeu est fait, rien ne vas plus," with such deep tones, and in such a monotonous manner, that it reminded me of poor little Paul Dombey at Dr. Blimber's school, when the clock continually repeated the doctor's question, "How-do-you-do, my-little-friend?"

Hamburg is beautifully situated, with pleasant walks and drives all about its neighborhood; and while many bodily cures are undoubtedly effected here, it is equally certain that many fortunes take wings across the green cloth, and are swallowed up in the capacious jaws of the bank.

Cologne, August 10.

A lovely day found us on the majestic Rhine, which with its ruined castles standing like silent sentinels on its heights, its vineyards, crags and mountains, presented a constantly changing picture, a "blending of all beauties," which we enjoyed extremely. The fortress of Ehrenbretstein opposite Coblentz, with which it is connected by a bridge of boats, is a massive and commanding structure, and seems perfectly invulnerable. It is almost entirely hewn out of the natural rock, and its resources are wonderful, it being capable of holding a garrison of fourteen thousand men, and the magazines are large enough to contain provisions for eight thousand men for ten years. It is, indeed, a stupendous fortification, towering majestically above everything else, and may well be called a "tower of victory."

The picturesque castle of Stolzenfels, which stands very high upon a jutting rock overlooking the Rhine, also justifies its name, "Proud Rock," by its commanding position, and truly regal appearance. With its ivy-covered battlements, turrets and towers, it is said to be the most imposing of all the castles on the Rhine. It was here that Queen Victoria and Prince Albert paid a visit some years ago to the King of Prussia. Shortly after passing it, we met a steamboat profusely decorated with British and Prussian flags, on which was the Prince of Wales, bound for the same charming place, to visit his sister, the Princess of Prussia. We reached Cologne late in the evening, after a day of constant and eager devotion to the beauties of the Rhine, which we thought *almost* equal to our own noble Hudson—but not quite. The captain of the steamboat, a young man of much intelligence, consoled us when we mentioned our lack of ruins, by saying, "Ah, but you do not *need* them!" He was right.

After a night's rest, we were prepared to visit the grand and beautiful Cologne Cathedral, which was commenced six hundred years ago, and is not yet finished. Workmen are employed to arrest the decay which has been going on for centuries, and others are adding their skill to the already exquisite workmanship evident everywhere. Yet it seems almost a hopeless task ever to finish the structure, although there is now a general interest felt in its completion all over Europe. Its gray buttresses are draped with verdure, vines and briars everywhere feed on its decay, ivy and moss overrun its walls in many places, while swallows and other birds build their nests amid the sculpture of its arches. But this decay is less evident within, as there are magnificent painted windows of modern date, and the vast pillars and arches are very imposing. The choir is very beautiful, with its rich painted windows of the fourteenth century, tapestries after designs by Rubens, frescoes, pillars, chapels and statues of the Apostles in colored and golden robes. Behind the high altar is the shrine of the three kings of Cologne—the wise men led by the star of Bethlehem to the manger where the infant Saviour lay. Through an opening in the shrine, the three skulls are seen, crowned with golden crowns ; their names, Gaspar, Melchior, and Balthazar, being written in rubies. They are most curious and ghastly relics, but are looked upon with entire faith by devout Catholics.

Santa Maria in Capitolio, which occupies the site of the capitol of the Roman city, is one of the oldest churches in Cologne. It dates from the year one thousand, and is placed upon the same spot on which a church was founded in the year seven hundred. We descended into the ancient crypt, which was once used as a place of worship, the walls of which are still covered with old paintings, and everything in perfect repair.

Cologne abounds in historical associations, and has much to interest in the way of pictures and antiquities. The Town Hall is a noble old building, having been erected in different centuries, and combining the Gothic and Italian styles. We felt, in walking about, that whatever might have been the state of Cologne in the days of Coleridge, it hardly deserved the reputation he has given it by the well-known lines :

> " The river Rhine, it is well known,
> Doth wash your city of Cologne ;
> But tell me, nymphs, what power divine
> Shall henceforth wash the river Rhine ?"

Certainly, the river Rhine can wash it now, and not need *much* cleansing. Perhaps the reputation for vile odors may have been an advantage to the various manufacturers of Eau de Cologne, of which there are twenty and more who claim to be the veritable successor of the inventor, Jean Maria Farina himself. Of one of these unmistakable personages we made a purchase, which quite satisfied us, although we were by no means sure that his was the genuine article, after all. One cannot buy of all the competitors, however, and must exercise much faith.

Brussells.

Our journey of several hours to the gay little capital of Belgium, was warm and uncomfortable, and the drive from the railway station to the pleasant Hotel de Bellevue, in the Place Royale, seemed interminable. We found ourselves near a park, rich in grand old trees, and adorned with statuary. The house itself had been made famous in the revolution of eighteen hundred and thirty, by being in the midst of the combat between the Dutch troops and Belgian insurgents. It was riddled with shot, and for a long time, many of the cannon balls were allowed to remain imbedded in the walls ; but it is a peaceful, quiet place, now, and thoroughly comfortable. In the centre of the square in front of the hotel is a spirited horse, in bronze, which looks ready to leap from his pedestal, with his rider, Godfrey of Bouillon. One could not but think of the different scenes that square must have presented after the battle of Waterloo, when the poor wounded soldiers were carried by hundreds through it. The city now is so bright, gay and cheerful, so like a Paris in miniature, that it is difficult to associate such scenes of misery with it.

When we visited the lace manufactory, however, for which Brussells is so famous, we felt that we were in a scene of misery in one sense, although the fabric shown us was so exquisitely beautiful. Brussells lace loses much of its beauty when one learns that those who spin the thread are obliged to work in close, dark rooms, into which the light is admitted through a small aperture, thus requiring such careful attention as to make the effort very painful. Those who make the lace are all rendered near-sighted by the nature of the labor, and frequently lose their sight entirely. Most of the poor creatures whom we saw at work, looked sad and dispirited, and we did not wonder, when we saw them straining their eyes over the delicate meshes. They sometimes work steadily for days, on a single flower or leaf; and the lace is kept unsoiled by being constantly covered, except at the point on which they are immediately engaged. It was a striking commentary on the business that a box was placed in the workroom, for the contribution of visitors towards the support of those who had become blind, or disabled by the work; and it was something of a relief to our consciences, to bestow our mite, after making a purchase.

The Cathedral of St. Gudule is a very handsome Gothic edifice, with splendid painted glass windows, and statues of the twelve apostles placed against the pillars in the nave. There are also some monuments to the Dukes of Brabant, one of them being a lion in bronze. The pulpit is a masterpiece of wood carving, by Verbruggen ; and the more we examined its minuteness and perfection of finish, the more remarkable it seemed. "It represents a globe supported on the tree of knowledge of good and evil. At the base of the tree, Adam and Eve are being driven out of Paradise by an angel, who wields the sword of flame ; while Death, as a sheeted skeleton, glides around with his dart, from the other side. The tree is teeming with delicious-looking fruit, and perched on the branches are many birds and animals. At the side of Adam are the ostrich and the eagle, while, in rather satirical vicinity to Eve, appear the ape, the peacock and the parrot. Above the canopy stands the Virgin, bearing the infant Saviour in her arms, and assisting to thrust the extremity of the cross into the serpent's head." The pulpit is certainly a sermon in itself, and it is doubtful if more eloquent ones are often preached from it.

We found much to admire in the way of paintings, in the old Palace of the Prince of Orange, and looked with great interest upon the grand Hotel de Ville, situated in a grand old square. It was finished in fourteen hundred and forty-two, and is said to be the most splendid municipal palace in the Netherlands. The abdication of Charles V. took place here, and in the market-place in front, the Counts Egmont and Horn were beheaded by order of the cruel Alva, in fifteen hundred and sixty-eight. From the windows of an old Gothic house in front of the square, Alva is said to have looked down on the execution. The beautiful tower of Gothic open-work, upon the Hotel de Ville, is surmounted by a copper figure of St. Michael, which is seventeen feet high, but seems no larger than an ordinary weathercock. The view from the spire is very extensive, and the colossal lion which marks the centre of the battle-field of Waterloo is easily seen from it. The house, too, which Lord Byron has made so memorable, where the Duchess of Gordon gave the grand ball on the eve of that wonderful battle, is still standing—but the "beauty and the chivalry" of that occasion have long since passed away.

Paris, September 3.

We have spent three charming weeks in this most charming city, and begin to feel that we have seen a *little* of Paris—but only a little, compared with what remains to be seen. We have wandered through the immense palace of the

Louvre, with its seven miles of pictures—its sculptures, relics, models, costumes of all times and lands, and personal memorials of nearly all the French monarchs. Among the latter, a valuable cabinet, belonging to Marie Antoinette, and the veritable gray coat and three-cornered hat which one so frequently sees in the portraits of Napoleon I. One feels almost oppressed by the vastness and richness of the collection.

At Versailles, we literally *skated* through the galleries, the floors being so highly polished as to render the effort of walking almost painful. We found much to interest us in the portraits of distinguished characters of France, and laughed heartily over the caricatures of our own Washington, and other American celebrities, which were hanging in state in one of the rooms.

The collection of battle-pieces by Horace Vernet, Paul de la Roche, and numerous others, is something wonderful, and would require weeks to examine. Among the sculptures, the admirable statue of Joan of Arc, by the Princess Marie of Orleans, the daughter of Louis Philippe, seemed a remarkable specimen of artistic skill—remarkable, at least, for *royal* hands.

We found the gardens and park, with their

numerous fountains, statues, and vases, most enchanting ; and it was pleasant to see everywhere the merry groups who were enjoying it all to their hearts' content.

The Grand Trianon, which is a handsome villa erected by Louis XIV. for Madame de Maintenon, contains some sumptuous apartments; while the Petite Trianon is simple, but tasteful, and infinitely more interesting from its having been the favorite resort of Marie Antoinette. The windows open upon a beautiful garden, and one could imagine what a charming retreat it must have been from the ceremonious life of royalty. We found it a striking contrast a few days after, to visit the low, brick-paved apartment of the Conciergerie, where for seventy-six days, after her husband had been beheaded, and her children torn away from her, she was tortured by misery, grief and humiliation. From this gloomy apartment she went to the guillotine, and we looked with sad interest upon the abode of such wretchedness. Upon a little altar in the room, is the small bronze crucifix which she used, and there are three pictures upon the wall, representing some of the closing scenes in her life—otherwise the room is empty and desolate.

One could almost imagine the noble woman, in her simple white dress, walking through the low door for the last time, with the majestic step which never faltered, presenting to the morning air her head turned gray by sorrow. One shuddered to think of the noble, refined woman, placed upon a common cart, her hands tied behind her, while the vulgar mob leered and jeered, followed her to the place of execution, and taunted her in her agonies; even stopping the cart in front of her palace, that she might be still farther agonized at seeing her former home, now so desolate.

Near the Conciergerie is the building occupied by the Prefecture de Police, and from this point emanates all the threads of the visible and invisible net-work of police authority. Public security is so admirably provided for in Paris that we were not sorry to see this building, although we found a discouraging amount of circumlocution necessary, in order to reach the Prefect, through whose permission alone we were allowed to visit the Conciergerie.

We met hosts of policemen, both in uniform and in citizens' dress, in our amusing wanderings up-stairs and down-stairs, to find the Prefect's chamber, and were almost afraid of being arrested for vagrants before our efforts were crowned with success.

We made a short visit to the Palais de Justice, and saw the judges and advocates in their black robes, pacing up and down the long, lofty hall, through which most of the courts are entered. The Sainte Chapelle, near by, was originally the palace chapel, and erected in twelve hundred and forty-five, for the reception of sacred relics. The interior consists of two chapels, an upper and a lower — the former having been destened for the accommodation of the court, the latter for the attendants. The Chapel is a very beautiful Gothic edifice, and in the upper chapel are clusters of columns, rich decorations, and gorgeous stained-glass windows of ancient date, which are placed so near together that the sides and ends seem entirely of glass. The effect is very rich and elegant.

We were very much delighted with the Jardin des Plantes, where all classes of objects belonging to Natural History are represented. The gardens are tastefully laid out, and an endless variety of living plants, animals and birds, are to be found there, while in the buildings that surround the garden are immense cabinets of botany, mineralogy, zoology, and comparative anatomy. There are free lectures given by different professors on all subjects connected with the kingdom of nature, in a large amphitheatre, which is capable of containing twelve thousand persons.

In the early part of this century, Humboldt presented four thousand five hundred tropical plants, which he had brought from America—three thousand of which belonged to species hitherto unknown. We rested some time beneath a magnificent cedar of Lebanon, which was planted there in seventeen hundred and thirty-five, while the celebrated Buffon was director of the gardens. Our drive through the beautiful Bois de Vincennes, which was formerly an ancient forest, and as early as twelve hundred a favorite hunting-ground of the French monarchs, was charming. It has been quite recently laid out as a Park, in the same style as the Bois de Bologne, and will, one day, rival it in beauty. The chateau of Vincennes is very picturesque and interesting, from the many historical associations connected with it for hundreds of years, and the long list of illustrious persons confined within its walls. It is now used as an armory, and contains weapons for the equipment of one hundred and twenty thousand men. The wonderful collection of curiosities in the Hotel Cluny, astonished and delighted us, as well as the quaint building itself. The curiosities exceed three thousand in number, and are of endless variety. There are carvings, ecclesiastical decorations and vestments, furniture, tapestry, weapons, carved ivory, stained glass, pictures, etc. One room is called "La Chambre de la Reine Blanche," because Mary, sister of Henry VIII. of England, and widow of Louis XII., once occupied it, and wore white mourning according to the custom of the Queens of England. It contains now a variety of musical instruments of olden times—among them the earliest style of piano, a little thing on slender legs, very different from the grand and massive ones now in use.

Through the back court one enters the lofty, vaulted hall, which constitutes the only remnant of the old Roman baths. It seems a strange thing to find *there,* and with the curiosities it contains, is the only specimen of the old Roman period existing in Paris.

We have been fortunate in being in Paris during the fête in honor of the birthday of

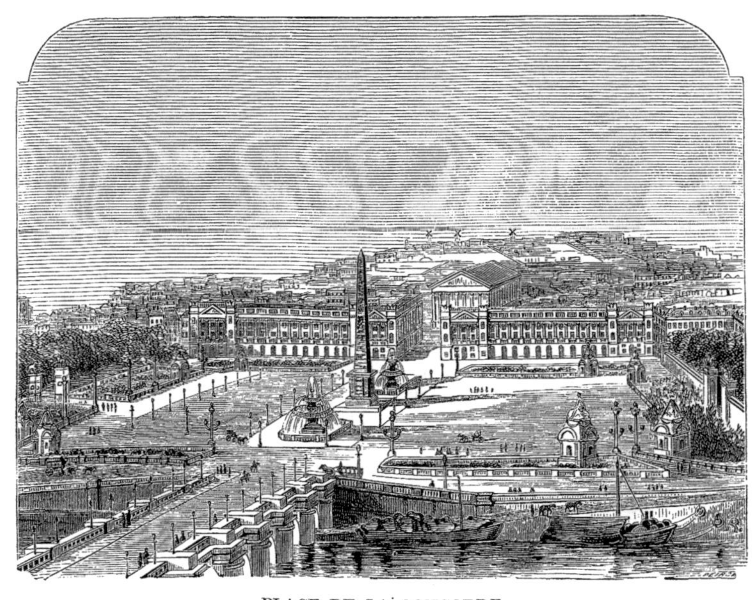

PLACE DE LA CONCORDE.

Napoleon I., which occurs on the fifteenth of August. The illumination, decorations, and fire-works were very grand and imposing, and the military display very fine. The Emperor rode up and down the ranks reviewing the troops, followed by the Prince Imperial, who touched his cap gracefully to the thousands of people who stood to the right and left, looking on. There did not seem to be much enthusiasm, however, and we only heard "Vive l'Emperor," now and then. One could not but look with deep interest on the pretty little boy, and wonder what the future had in store for him. We afterwards saw the Empress, and were sorry to notice a care-worn expression on her still beautiful face; but her life must necessarily be one of great anxiety, and of late, the health of her only child has been an added sorrow to her loving heart. He *looked* very robust, however. The scene in the Place de la Concorde, in the evening, was magnificent. The place itself, with the beautiful trees of the Tuilleries on one side, the Champs Elysées opposite, the two fountains, the obelisk of Luxor, the groups and single statues, all were brilliantly illuminated. The entire length of the Champs Elysées to the

Arc de Triomphe was a scene of enchantment—rows of lamps on each side making the whole distance as light as noon-day, and showing the outline of the arch with entire distinctness. From the Tuilleries garden to the Arc de Triomphe there was a dense crowd of people—men, women and children—and it is difficult to imagine a more animated, or more beautiful scene. The fête finished with some gorgeous fire-works, which seemed to illuminate the whole heavens. Notwithstanding the immense crowd, everything passed off very quietly and harmoniously, and the Police had little to do but look on.

We have seen more of our own Protestant churches in Paris than any others, but the Madeleine and Notre Dame claimed our notice, and the former seemed to us very unchurchlike, although very magnificent. It is wholly of marble, without and within, and its form is that of a Grecian Temple, it having been designed by Napoleon I. as a "Temple of Glory." Afterwards the distinction of the edifice was altered by Louis XVIII. who proposed to convert it into an expiatory church to the memory of Louis XVI., Louis XVII., Marie Antionette, and Madame Elizabeth. The restored Bourbon dynasty made it a church, and it was completed under Louis Philippe, with an inscription on the front which dedicated it "to the Almighty God, through the invocation of St. Mary Magdalene." The Corinthian colonnade by which it is surrounded, with its magnificent cornice and colossal figures of saints between the columns, all make it very grand. There are no windows, but the light enters through four sky-lights which surmount cupolas, very gorgeously gilded. This, however, prevents many of the pictures and statues from being seen to the best advantage, as the light is insufficient. All the chapels are decorated with statues of their different patron saints, and *pictures* representing scenes from the life of Mary Magdalene. The Chapelle des Mariages contains a group in marble representing the nuptials of the Virgin; and the Chapelle des Fonts, or baptismal chapel, is adorned with a group representing Christ and John the Baptist in the Jordan. The interior is a spacious hall, richly decorated and gilded, and very beautiful, but does not suggest a temple of worship.

Notre Dame is a fine Gothic structure of a very different character. It stands on an island in the Seine, and is surrounded by sheds and workshops, which do not add to its beauty, but its three arched portals, with their exquisite sculptures, are very fine. The three rose windows of ancient stained glass are considered the most beautiful in Europe; but the effect of the interior has been sadly injured by the recent painting of the various chapels, in genuine wall-paper patterns. This church will always be interesting from the associations connected with it—Napoleon I. having been married here to Josephine, and the present Emperor to the present Empress. On the occasion of the baptism of the Prince Imperial, the ceiling was decorated with golden stars on a blue ground. This, however, has been removed, although the present taste is very questionable.

We have, of course, indulged in the "round of shopping" which seems to be considered essential to a thorough understanding of Paris, and while we have found the shops abundantly supplied with the most elegant articles, we have *not* found

> "All manner of things that a woman can put
> On the crown of her head, or the sole of her foot,"

so *very* cheap. Certain things in the way of finery may be cheaper, but anything substantially elegant, is costly. Still, there is no doubt that the same thing would be more expensive in

NOTRE DAME.

our own land; so that when one is in Paris, it is better to take advantage of that fact. Then there is an *air* about anything made by a Parisian modiste, which it is difficult for any one else to acquire, for the French seem to have a magic power in matters of dress.

Newport, Isle of Wight, Sept. 7.

There could not well be a greater change than from gay, bustling Paris to this quiet old town. Our journey here was most agreeably varied by a short visit to Rouen and Havre. In the former place, we went first to the Cathedral, a splendid monument of Gothic architecture, containing many fine sculptures and monuments; among them the tomb of Richard Cœur de Lion, whose heart is buried in the Cathedral, he having bequeathed it to the city of Rouen, on account of the great love he bore the Normans.

The church of St. Ouen is much superior to the Cathedral in point of size and architectural beauty, although having less historic monuments. The central tower is very elegant, being nearly three hundred feet high, and of most graceful proportions, while the interior is a "perfect pattern of airy gracefulness." We were delighted with our drive through the quaint streets of

Rouen, with its most curious old gateways and elaborately carved dwellings. The Place de la Pucelle, took us back to the thirtieth of July, fourteen hundred and thirty-one, when Joan of Arc, the glorious shepherd girl that had delivered France, was burned at the stake. A monument is erected to her memory, to mark the place where she suffered. And *here* that young girl of twenty was burned for heresy, with a soldier's staff broken, and formed into a rough cross, clasped to her breast; while her meek and saintly demeanor won from her enemies, that till now had believed her a witch, tears of rapturous admiration. And when the smoke was rising upwards in volumes, and she saw that the one friend that would not forsake her, a Dominican monk, who was praying at her side, was in danger, she thought only of *him*, bidding him with her last breath to care for his own preservation, but to leave her to God.

It is not strange that the executioner knelt at every shrine for pardon for his share in this awful tragedy! Now, it is said that the Bishop of Orleans seriously intends to demand of the Pope, to canonize the heroic girl. How strange that a Church which in one century burns a woman at the stake as an instrument of the foul fiend, can, in another, proclaim that she was a saint; and that pious Catholics must tell their beads before her statue to the supplication, "Saint Joan of Arc! pray for us!"

The fact that Havre was a seaport town, seemed to reveal itself everywhere we went; and we found the collections of shells and corals in the shops very attractive. It seemed to us that every shop was a depository for various articles pertaining to the sea. Few things, however, interested us so much as the wonderful aquarium in the gardens of the Exposition, which is most admirably managed, and contains a great variety of fish and beautiful sea plants. The light coming from above, upon the large glass tanks containing them, added very much to the effect, and we wandered about among these "wonders of the deep" for a long time with great delight.

Our voyage from Havre to Southampton was made in one of the elegant and commodious steamers with which travellers are accommodated in crossing the channel! The spacious saloon was hardly large enough to "swing a cat" in; and although like Mr. Dick in David Copperfield, I could say, "I don't want to swing a cat, I never do swing a cat; therefore, what does that signify to *me!*" yet I found it *did* signify, so I resigned my right in the crowded cabin, and very thankfully took a position on deck for the night. With a glorious full moon, and the sea without a ripple, the night passed most comfortably, and we were all prepared to sing again the praises of the Channel, over which we had passed twice with such entire comfort.

We remained in Southampton only long enough to walk from one steamer to another, and after a pleasant sail of an hour, found ourselves at Cowes on the Isle of Wight, from which place to Newport was only a short expedition by rail. The Isle of Wight has been called a miniature England, and it certainly seems to have the exquisite finish which only a master hand can give. The afternoon of our arrival, we drove to Carisbrook Castle, in which Charles I. was imprisoned during the troublous times of Cromwell and the Commonwealth. The window from which he attempted to escape is still shown; and one could not look from it, and think of his sad fate, without a feeling of sorrowful sympathy. The castle is most charmingly situated, commanding views in all directions, of hills, dales, woods and gentlemen's villas. We wandered about the walls, looking through the openings, and climbing to the top of the keep, where we sat for a long time enjoying the beauty of the scene. Below us was the old tournament ground, and it required but a little imagination to bring before us the gay cavaliers, and bright-eyed ladies, who once graced that spot. The famous well of the Castle, which is two hundred and ten feet deep, and twelve wide, is very remarkable, and the trained donkey which draws the water stepped upon the wheel and kept it in motion until the bucket was raised, quite as if he considered it a matter of course. The immense depth of the well is all the more wonderful when one considers that there are only twenty-five feet of masonry, and the rest is cut from the solid rock. When a pin is dropped into the well, the sound produced when it strikes the water is distinctly heard; and a candle let down, was almost lost to sight from the great distance it travelled before reaching the water.

Donkeys are quite an institution here, and we saw one meek-looking animal browsing quietly about, enjoying a green old age, which had worked faithfully at the windlass more than forty years.

On our return from the castle, we visited some curious Roman remains near Newport, which were discovered nine years ago. It has been supposed that a Roman villa once stood upon the spot, and some of the mosaic pavement is very perfect and entire. The woman in charge of the place amused us very much with her description of the various rooms originally there, going about with all the air of having resided there in the old Roman days, and pointing out each different apartment by saying "This *were* the kitchen—this *were* the court-yard," &c.

We have spent one day driving about the island and visiting the scene of Legh Richmond's labors—a day long to be remembered. On our way to Brading we went to one of the extensive chalk-pits for which the island is so famous, and it seemed strange to stand upon the brink of a precipice formed entirely of the soft, pure material. The bright sun upon it made it quite unpleasantly dazzling to the eye. Shortly after, we ascended a hill and sat down on the ground near the triangular stone pyramid where Legh Richmond so often sat, when his mind was "filled with any interesting subject for meditation." It was pleasant to look upon the same glorious scenes which had charmed *him* so often, and we found, indeed, a "complete circle of interesting objects," comprising every variety of beautiful and magnificent views. Hills covered with corn, grass, wood, heath or fern—a river running through fruitful valleys—villages, churches, country-seats, farm-houses and cottages, were scattered in every direction, while far off appeared the ocean glittering in the sunlight. We spent some time on this favorite "mount for contemplation," and then drove to the old church in Brading where Legh Richmond so faithfully labored. The church is an antique structure of the seventh century, and the parsonage formerly stood at the end of the church-yard, but has been taken down. The trees under which he used to assemble his little group, are still standing, and we could imagine them dispersed in the church-yard, learning the verses he desired. "Little Jane, the young cottager," is buried near the church, and the stone is still to be seen with the epitaph she learned, which so much impressed her. Few churches are visited with more interest than this simple, unpretending structure, which brings travellers from all parts of the world—Legh Richmond's tracts having been translated into nearly every European language.

We drove to Sandown, a pretty bathing-place on the sea, and were quite amused in watching the small houses drawn out into the water by a single horse, into which ladies entered on the shore, handsomely bedecked, and soon appeared at the rear of the house, plunging into the waves, and looking very much like escaped lunatics.

From Sandown we drove to the beautiful village of Shanklin, and walked through Shanklin Chine, a curious opening in the cliff, through which a stream of water runs, the steep descending sides being covered with trees, bushes, wild-flowers and ferns, while occasionally bold masses of rocks appear. It is the wildest, prettiest place imaginable, with views of the ocean, now and then, which were magnificent. At the upper extremity of this great fissure, some picturesque cottages, covered with ivy, are placed, and near one, a pretty rustic fountain asked us to partake of its cooling water, by an inscription rudely printed upon it :

> O, traveller, stay thy weary feet ;
> Drink of this fountain, cool and sweet ;
> It flows for rich and poor the same.

Then go thy way, remembering still
The wayside well beneath the hill,
The cup of water in his name.'

Such an invitation was irresistible, and we found the pure element most refreshing after our long tramp.

Our drive to Heal Common, the former home of the Dairyman's Daughter, added another pleasure to our pleasant day. The cottage stands as it did in the days of the Walbridge family, but *they* have long since passed away. The house still wears the old aspect of neatness, and the little dairy, with its stone floor, bright rows of tins, and fresh pats of butter, looked very inviting, but the little, low chamber, where Elizabeth Walbridge's weary hours of suffering were made bright and peaceful by her Christian faith, was more interesting than all. One could almost imagine the pale face lying upon that pillow, and the feeble voice uttering her last words—"All is well, well, well."

We went to the old church of Arreton, with its dial on the wall, where she was buried on the thirtieth of May, eighteen hundred and one. It is a curious specimen of olden time, with tablets inserted in the walls, and upon the pillars, while the churchyard in which it stands is filled with crumbling tombstones and quaint epitaphs. One individual, who had left a yearly sum to the poor, is thus commemorated on one of the church tablets:

"Loe here under this tombe incoutcht
  Is William Serle by name;
Who for his deeds of charitie
  Deserveth worthy fame.
A man within this Parish borne,
  And in the house called Stone
A glasse for to behold a work
  Hath left to every one;
For that unto the people pore
  Of Arreton he gave
An hundred powndes in redie coyne
  He willed that they shoold have
To be employed in fittest sorte
  As man coold best invent
For yearly relief to the pore,
  That was his good intent;
Thus did this man, a batcheler,
  Of years full fifty-nyne,
And doeinge good to many a one,
  Soe did he spend his tyme,
Until the days he did decease,
  The first of Februarey,
And in the yeare of One Thousand
  Five hundred neyntie-five."

We have been made very comfortable at the Bugle Hotel in Newport, and are quite willing to sound its praise in loud and earnest tones.

Indeed, there are few days that better deserve a "white stone," than those we have passed on the lovely Isle of Wight.

London, September 11.

We find London comparatively quiet and deserted at this unfashionable season, and it seems to have lost many of its charms since we left, last May. But we have found much to interest us, nevertheless, and our visit to the National Museum at South Kensington was a source of great pleasure, not only for the immense collections in the way of botany, models, drawings, china, etc., but the numerous fine paintings to be seen there. The buildings are on the most extensive scale, and admirably arranged; and it was a great pleasure to look upon the originals of so many pictures long familiar to us in engravings. The gallery is rich in paintings by Hogarth, Sir Joshua Reynolds, Copley, Sir Benjamin West, Turner, and Landseer. It abounds in portraits of distinguished personages, and we stood for a long time before those of John Philip Kemble and Mrs. Siddons, by Sir Thomas Lawrence. The former is superbly dressed as Hamlet, while the latter wears the short waist of the day, with her arms bare to the shoulders—the beautiful arms, on which it is said that Sir Thomas Lawrence employed sixty hours. The famous Cartoons of Raphael, which were originally made for designs in tapestry for the Vatican, and are described as "not excelled in beauty and completeness by any paintings in existence," are now at Kensington, after a sojourn of many years at Hampton Court. One only wonders that they should be in such a perfect state of preservation, after so long a time, and so many changes. We paid a pleasant visit to Christ's Hospital, or the Blue-Coat School, one day ; and while we could not but appreciate the noble charity which thus educates and maintains sometimes twelve hundred boys at once, we felt sorry for the poor fellows in the cruelly grotesque apparel prescribed for them, at the founding of the school, more than three hundred years ago. A long blue cloth coat, reaching nearly to their heels, an orange-colored short petticoat, a red leather belt, yellow stockings, and white bands, may have been considered *the thing* centuries ago, but now it looks strangely enough. The funny little woollen cap belonging to this costume, is about the circumference of a small saucer, has a tassel on the top, and no rim, fits the head quite snugly, and is carried in the *pocket.* We constantly met the boys in various parts of the city, and they were always bare-headed ; and we were told that even in winter they preferred the covering which nature has given their heads, to the prescribed caps. They find the long blue coat very much in their way sometimes, and we were quite amused with their ingenuity in tucking it up under their belts when at play, thus making an odd-looking short jacket of it. Everything in the hospital is in beautiful order and thoroughly comfortable.

Numerous portraits of Edward VI., the young boy-king who founded the institution, embellish the walls, and we walked about thinking of Charles Lamb, and other men of world-wide fame, who had made these corridors ring with their merry laughter.

On the last day of our stay in London we made a pilgrimage to the Tower, one of the most remarkable places there, it having been at different times, a strong fortress, a splendid palace, a secure prison, and associated with the history of the past, for centuries. The first part was built by William the Conqueror, in ten hundred and seventy-six, as a safe place of retreat for himself and his followers in case of a revolt against him by the citizens of London. The Tower is now a confused cluster of buildings, each having its own history. It is manned by a considerable body of troops, and contains the principal supply of arms for the army and navy. It was wonderful to see the artistic skill with which these arms are arranged on the walls and ceilings of large halls, the glittering weapons being formed in every design imaginable. In one long gallery, there are wooden horses in full plate armor, as large as life, on which are seated figures of knights and nobles, also in full armor, as if ready for battle. In many instances the squire, similarly encased, stands at his master's side. The effect on first entering this hall, with all these knights arranged as if in battle array, and armed to the teeth, is quite startling. Then there are suits of steel and chain armor that once belonged to English kings, and specimens of antique and foreign weapons. In one apartment are thumbscrews, racks, instruments of torture, and the block and axe used for the execution of the two wives of Henry VIII. and Lady Jane Grey. We thought of the golden canopy drawn by many horses covered with white damask, under which poor Anne Boleyn was seated when taken to the Tower in grand procession, a beautiful young bride, courted and caressed. In less than four years, that fair young head lay upon the bloody block before us. We found much to make us shudder in the Tower, and much to make us rejoice that those days of tyranny were over. We were shown the room which for many centuries was used for state prisoners, with inscriptions still remaining upon its walls, made by its various heart-broken inmates—the tower in which the Princess Elizabeth was imprisoned, and the octagonal room in which Sir Walter Raleigh was confined for twelve years, with his bed-room excavated in the prison wall, which is here seventeen feet thick. Here he wrote his "History of the World," and from here he went to the block, saying, "It matters not how a man's head lies, so that his heart is right." The man in the crowd seems to have spoken the truth, who said, when Raleigh's head fell from his shoulders, "We have not such another head to cut off."

Of course, among the wonders of the Tower, we peeped at the Crown Jewels, after being locked in the room before we were allowed to do so. They are placed in a large glass case in the centre of the room, and an iron railing prevents any person from coming too near them. They can be seen, however, without any difficulty, and the display was very fine, comprising some of the crowns worn by the kings and queens of past generations, and that of the present queen, which is composed of purple velvet, enclosed by hoops of silver, and studded with diamonds, rubies and sapphires. As it weighs a pound and three-quarters, it is not strange that the queen seldom wears it.

The famous Ko-ih-noor, or mountain-of-light diamond, is also in the case, with many other gems and articles of value—among them, the silver gilt baptismal font, in which some of the royal babies have been baptized. We have taken great pleasure in seeking out the spots so interesting to an American, associated with the great and good who have passed away, with whose names we are so familiar. The old churches, too, are full of interest to us, and we feel that London has a dignity peculiarly its own. It is not so gay as the continental cities we have just left, but is solid, substantial, and elegant, and the more one sees of it, the more one admires it.

Leamington, September 14.

We tarried a few hours at Oxford on our way here, and although we had not time to visit the twenty colleges and five halls, which constitute the University, we were able to see the most famous of them all, Christ College, which owes its origin to Cardinal Wolsey. In the chapel, which is also the cathedral church of the bishopric of Oxford, are some ancient and curious monuments, and the church itself is a most quaint specimen of a past age. The dining-hall, said to be the finest in the kingdom, is decorated with an extensive collection of portraits, and the library is very rich in manuscripts, prints and coins. Everything looked old and quaint, but it was so well kept, and in such perfect order, that it was a great pleasure to roam about through the different courts and corridors, and over the green lawns. We drove to the Theatre, where degrees are conferred—an immense building with galleries, which was designed by Sir Christopher Wren.

It is here that the students make merry on "commemoration day," and take such liberties with the dignitaries assembled there—last year saying to Mr. Tennyson when he walked in, dressed somewhat carelessly, "Did your mother call you early, Mr. Tennyson?" Degrees are conferred here; and many, like Robert Southey, have been "Ell ell deed," after being called "many laudatory names ending in issimus."

The view of Oxford and its surroundings, from the top of the theatre, quite repaid us for the ascent, and we afterwards drove to the rivers Isis and Churwell, on which Oxford is situated, and saw the gayly-painted crafts which make the boat races there so famous. The Martyrs' Memorial also interested us very much, standing as it does upon the spot where Cranmer, Ridley and Latimer met their fate with such wonderful serenity—the former holding the hand which had unwillingly signed a recantation of his principles, over the flames, saying, "Oh, this unworthy hand—this unworthy hand!" The monument was erected by public subscription in eighteen hundred and forty-one, and there are statues of the martyrs standing in niches upon it. The inscription says that "they yielded their bodies to be burned, rejoicing that to them it was given, not only to believe in Christ, but also to suffer for his sake."

We have been most comfortably situated at the

Regent's Hotel in Leamington, and have found the drives in this lovely Warwickshire very delightful. Hearing that the Earl of Warwick was expected the night of our arrival, and that it would be impossible to gain an entrance into the castle during his residence there, we drove to it almost immediately. The grand old castle, situated on a rock washed by the river Avon, is very magnificent, and we strolled through its long suites of apartments adorned with valuable paintings, rich furniture, vases, statues, and all sorts of beautiful and costly things, not knowing which to admire most, the wonderful collection within, or the glorious views seen without, from each window. The grand entrance hall, which is sixty-two feet long, and forty wide, has a floor of polished marble, and a ceiling of beautifully carved oak. It is hung with shining suits of armor, great branching horns of deer, and has a deep, wide chimney, where we could fancy the Yule log burning at gay Christmas gatherings, while the wassail cup passed merrily round. We lingered under the magnificent oaks and cedars in the grounds, saw the beautiful antique vase found near Hadrian's villa at Tivoli, which holds one hundred and sixty-eight gallons—and again passed through the long, wide passage cut in the rock, lined with ivy and flowers, through which we entered the grounds of the castle. Here we saw, in the porter's lodge, the armor of Guy of Warwick, the gigantic man who carried a sword seven feet long, and weighing twenty pounds, and wore helmet, shield and breast-plate, to match. His porridge-pot, which holds one hundred and two gallons, and from which it is said he was accustomed to take his food, is filled with punch on grand occasions, and distributed to the tenantry.

We left the castle carrying in our minds pictures of beauty not soon forgotten. Among the paintings upon the walls, the grand portrait of Charles I. by Vandyke, which hangs by itself at the end of a narrow hall, impressed us most. From Warwick we drove to Kenilworth, once a lordly structure, and now a beautiful and picturesque ruin. We wandered among its yet unlevelled walls and towers covered with ivy, and thought of the visit of Queen Bess in fifteen hundred and seventy-five, when she entered in grand procession, escorted by her favorite Earl of Leicester, and followed by her brilliant court. During the seventeen days of her visit, what a scene of revelry must that castle have been—each day having its special sports. Hunting, dancing, bear-baiting, Italian tumblers, donkey-racing, tilting, &c., to say nothing of eating and drinking, were constantly going on. Now these magnificent fêtes are over, and solemn-looking rooks are the principal dwellers here. "Where princes feasted and heroes fought, all is now desolate," yet very lovely in its desolation.

Our drive to Stratford on Avon was over a pleasant road, and we found it a pretty country town, quiet and sunny, with many new, modern-looking buildings in it which denote a present prosperity, while there are still a large number of quaint, moss-grown houses, which seem to belong to the far away past. It took us, indeed, far into the past, to tread the very pavements once trodden by Shakspeare, and to walk across the fields over which *he* had so often walked, in his early manhood, to visit his beloved Anne Hathaway. The old walls and dilapidated roof of the cottage still remain, and we stood in the immense fire-place and sat upon a worm-eaten settle on which we were told the lovers used to sit. But there are few things in the cottage connected either with the poet or his wife, although it is now occupied by a lineal descendant of the Hathaways. We were glad that the walk to Shottery was by a simple foot-path, and that we were compelled occasionally to cross a stile, for it all seemed to harmonize with one's poetic memories of Shakspeare. We could imagine the boy of eighteen, running merrily over the very path we were treading to "tell his love" to the fair one, who, after all, did not make him very happy. The old, unpretending house, with its three rooms, the front one having been a butcher's shop, where Shakspeare was born, is still kept as it was, with the exception of some necessary repairs. A narrow flight of winding, wooden stairs, leads into a low chamber, with one window looking out upon the quiet street, in which the greatest of all poets first saw the light of Heaven. The room is small and simple, yet the humble and great of all nations have there met to do homage to genius. Its walls, and the albums kept there, bear the names of the noblest in rank and talent that the world has seen.

For a century and a half after the poet's death, the house remained the property of private individuals; but it is now owned by the nation, and the garden and grounds in the rear have been made very attractive with trees, shrubs and flowers.

From the first home of Shakspeare we walked through the quiet streets to the picturesque old church on the banks of the Avon, where he was laid to his rest. The entrance is through a beautiful avenue of lime trees, the branches forming an arch overhead, and the church contains many gorgeous monuments, but the simple bust over a doörway in the chancel representing the poet writing upon a cushion, is more attractive than all. It is painted to resemble life—the eyes being a light hazel, the hair and beard auburn, the doublet scarlet, and the gown, without sleeves, black. His death in sixteen hundred and sixteen, and his age, fifty-three, are inscribed beneath the bust, while over the rough free-stone slab in the chancel, which covers his dust, are the famous lines which have kept the spot sacred from intrusion so long. We lingered a long time at this "pilgrim shrine," and then returned to the Red Horse Inn, which has been immortalized by our own countryman. We were shown into a parlor, over the door of which, "Washington Irving's parlor" was painted in large letters, and an iron poker was brought us, carefully treasured up in a crimson velvet bag, on which was engraved "Geoffrey Crayon"—it being the one which *he* used when there. It was pleasant to find our great prose writer remembered in the home of the great poet.

On our return to Leamington we drove by Charlecote Hall, which is about four miles from Stratford, and the scene of Shakspeare's trial for poaching. The house is a quaint old building in the Elizabethan style, and the parks filled with grand old trees, under which we saw immense herds of deers, showing that a taste for these pretty, graceful creatures still exists in the Lucy family. We also drove through the beautiful grounds of Stoneleigh Abbey, the country seat of Lord Leigh, charmingly situated on a sloping bank of the Avon, where we saw some ivy-mantled remains of the old abbey which was founded in eleven hundred and fifty-four.

Leamington, although one of the most fashionable watering-places in England, is delightfully quiet, and it is difficult to believe that it is a place of great resort. It is pleasantly situated on the river Leam, and the streets wide, clean and handsomely built up. The beautiful grounds of the Jephson gardens, the noble gift of the benevolent Dr. Jephson himself, are very attractive, being very spacious, and laid out with great taste. There are terraces, walks winding by the river, and miniature lake—a shadowy grove, open spaces for croquet and archery—flowers, summer-houses and rustic arbors—swans on the lake, a band of music in summer, and skating in the winter. Truly, as Mr. Hawthorn says, "Leamington seems always to be in flower, and serves as a home for the homeless all the year round." We did not find many persons in the pump-room in the morning, and when we had tasted the *beverage* we were not surprised.

Birmingham.

We have remained long enough in this smoky city to become somewhat initiated in the process of manufacturing some of the articles for which the town is famous. The beautiful papier maché manufacture, which commences with a coarse piece of paper, and by putting several thicknesses together and polishing, rubbing and painting, becomes an exquisite piece of furniture, interested us very much. Then we saw the electroplating, which speedily turns a common-looking article into something so like gold and silver, that it is impossible to detect the difference. Afterwards we went to the wonderful steel-pen manufactory of Joseph Gillott, and were astonished beyond measure to see how many hands a steel pen went through before it was finished, and how large and extensive Mr. Gillott's factories are. He gives employment to many hundred persons, and we were glad to see the workmen in pleasant, well-ventilated, and well-lighted rooms.

Peacock Inn, Derbyshire.

We are at the most perfect specimen of an old English inn that can be imagined; the favorite resort, as it may well be, of artists and anglers, and all who enjoy the picturesque and beautiful. The house itself, with its gabled roof, clustering chimneys, ivy-clad porch, and vine of brilliant berries, entirely covering the front, deserves the name of "pride of the village"—while its situation in a pretty garden, with a stream of water pattering over the pebbles at the foot, and an arched stone bridge near, is charming. The historic associations of olden time are manifest as one approaches the doorway, over which is the carved figure of an expanded peacock, the crest of the Manners' family. Below it are the mysterious letters

IOHNSTE
VENSON
1653.

which probably means that one John Stevenson was once the fortunate proprietor of this establishment.

Mr. Longfellow, who was here a few days ago, was very loth to leave this lovely spot, and we can fully appreciate his regret. It is a place to tarry in for weeks—not days. The scenery is charmingly picturesque, and we have greatly enjoyed our drives to Haddon Hall and Chatsworth; the former place taking us back to the old feudal times, and the latter showing the magnificence of the present. Haddon Hall is a complete picture of an ancient baronial residence, beautifully situated on an eminence on the east side of the river Wye, and as its ivy-clad towers rise majestically above the wood-crowned hills, the effect is very grand and imposing. For a century and a half, it has been occupied only by those who have the care of it, but it is kept in perfect repair, and is wholly unaltered since the days when it was a constant scene of hospitality and revelry. The kitchen is immense, having two fireplaces, each large enough to roast an ox whole, while there are double ranges of dressers, and irons for a multitude of spits. Large chopping blocks, and a massive wooden table hollowed out into basins for kneading-troughs, show that the seven score of servants formerly employed here were kept busy. The banqueting hall has a music gallery over the entrance, and at the opposite end of the room is the raised floor or dais, where the master of the house sat with his more distinguished guests, *above the salt,* which always occupied the centre of the board. Persons of inferior degree were stationed *below the salt,* thus denoting their rank. We were shown an iron handcuff, still chained to the wall, in which it was customary to lock the wrist of any guest who refused to take his portion of liquor. By this contrivance the hand was fastened very high above the head, and while in that position a quantity of cold water was poured down the sleeve of the unfortunate victim. Pleasant way that of making a man convivial! There is still another dining-room, which was fitted up, when it became less customary for the lord of the mansion to dine with his dependents. This was built in fifteen hundred and forty-five, and over the fire-place is a panel with the motto underneath

"Drede God and honour the Kyng." We were shown numerous rooms in this most interesting place, and all the principal ones were hung with loose arras, much of which remains. The doors were concealed behind the hangings, but there were great iron hooks by which the tapestry could be held back, to avoid the necessity of lifting it up every time, when passing in and out.

In one of the bed-chambers is preserved the once magnificent state bed, on which royal personages have often slept—George IV. having been the last occupant. The bed is richly decorated with green velvet, lined with white satin, and the now tattered canopy and hangings are said to have been embroidered in the reign of Henry VI. by Eleanor, the wife of Sir Robert Manners. The chapel is a most curious relic, showing distinctly by its architecture, that it was erected at different periods, and that personal comfort connected with religious worship, was unthought of in those days. The chapel contains some painted glass more than four centuries old, and on one window is an inscription in black-letter characters, suggesting a prayer for the souls of Richard Vernon and Benedicita his wife, by whom it was erected in fourteen hundred and twenty-seven. As we left this most remarkable of all the ancient houses in the kingdom, we saw, in one of the gardens belonging to the establishment, some very curious specimens of an art now almost out of use—the peculiar training and clipping of trees and shrubs to represent various figures. There was one clump of shrubbery cut to resemble a peacock, which was very perfect—the bill, crest and tail being complete.

From Haddon Hall we drove to Chatsworth, the "Palace of the Peak," which forms a striking contrast to the sombre aspect of the old baronial mansion we had just left, it being one of the "stately homes of England" of comparatively modern date, and in perfect repair. We drove a long distance through the park, with its glorious old trees, and herds of deer, until we reached the porter's lodge, with its three wrought iron, richly gilt gates. There we entered the court which leads to the great hall, a spacious and noble apartment, with a mosaic floor of black and white marble, and columns of beautiful Derbyshire spar. Over the fire-place is a tablet with the inscription, "These well-loved ancestral halls, founded in the year of English freedom, 1688, William Spencer, Duke of Devonshire, inherited in 1811, and perfected in the year of sorrow, 1840." The "year of sorrow" refers to the death of his wife.

We were conducted through apartments, with carved wainscoting, splendidly painted ceilings, inlaid oaken floors, exquisite statues, magnificent vases, long galleries of paintings and sculptures, until we were quite overpowered with the combination of genius, taste and skill.

Afterwards we walked about the grounds near the house, which are laid out with surpassing taste in every variety of landscape gardening. Immense rocks have been brought from a considerable distance, to make a formation of grotto work, having all the appearance of nature. Then there are fountains, artificial ponds, cascades, and a remarkable weeping willow, presenting all the appearance, in copper, of a living tree, which, on touching a spring, sends forth a shower of water from sprigs, leaves and roots. It is said that Queen Victoria (then Princess), after a visit to the Duke of Devonshire in eighteen hundred and thirty-two, when asked what she admired most at Chatsworth, replied, "the squirting tree!" We found the oak planted at that time by her youthful hands tall and thriving, and the

American chestnut which her illustrious mother, the Duchess of Kent placed in the ground on the same occasion, also in vigorous condition.

The conservatory, which has a passage in the centre large enough to drive a carriage through, and is covered by seventy-six thousand square feet of glass, contains the most rare and beautiful plants to be found, and an aquarium where water plants are raised in perfection. But with all the splendors within, and beauties without, the Duke of Devonshire only resides in this charming place a few weeks every year, having so many other residences which claim his attention. Truly, an "embarras des richesses." Nothing can be imagined more beautiful than the park, which is nine miles in circumference, and diversified with hill and dale.

York, September 17.

We reached this ancient city late last evening, and rose very early this morning to walk about the old walls, which have stood so firmly for centuries, and are still in a very perfect state. They are three miles in circumference, and have a delightful promenade on the top, which commands a beautiful prospect not only of the surrounding country, but the Minster, and Clifford's Tower, which was the old keep of the castle.

We felt quite like "pilgrims and strangers," as we took our early morning stroll, with the city so quiet beneath us—the "hum of multitudes astir," not having yet commenced. Fortunately, we found a verger who kindly admitted us into the magnificent cathedral, and we greatly enjoyed the early morning light upon it, and the sun shedding its rising beams upon the gorgeous stained glass east window of the Lady chapel, which has been called the "wonder of the world, both for masonry and glazing." We wandered about among the gigantic columns, and through the transept, nave, and beautiful choir, trying to comprehend the grandeur of this wondrous structure, but its magnificence was quite bewildering. So many hundred years have been spent in beautifying and perfecting it, that nothing seems wanting now.

Some of the old monuments are very peculiar. One of them is to the memory of Archbishop de Grey, who died in twelve hundred and fifty-five, and consists of a canopy, supported by black marble columns eight feet high. On a flat tomb under the canopy, is an effigy of the Archbishop in his pontifical robes.

But the splendors and beauties of this remarkable cathedral are endless, and we regretted that we could not go again and again, to enjoy, and wonder, and worship.

The ruins of St. Mary's Abbey, which was formerly a powerful monastic institution, founded in the time of William the Conqueror, are extremely pretty, although comparatively small. It was surrendered to Henry VIII. in fifteen hundred and forty, during the reformation, and there were then fifty monks in the establishment, enjoying its beauty and luxury.

Melrose, Scotland.

This pleasant village, picturesquely situated, as it is, on the Tweed, and at the base of the Eildon Hills, would have a charm in itself, but the elegant and graceful remains of its Abbey, so famous in romance and poetry, add greatly to its interest.

We are at the George Hotel, where an excellent portrait of Washington greeted us, as we entered the dining-room, and made us feel quite at home, at once.

We soon sought the beautiful ruins which have

MADELEINE.—[See Page 192.]

brought us here, and can, in some measure, imagine the ancient magnificence of this celebrated monastery, as it retains so much of its architectural splendor and sculptured beauty now, from the fact that the red sandstone of which it was built, has resisted the weather for ages—the minute ornaments are as entire as when newly wrought. When one remembers that it dates back as far as eleven hundred and thirty-six, and was destroyed in the sixteenth century, it seems indeed, wonderfully preserved.

We wandered about, enjoying the beautiful views at every point—the glorious windows, carvings, and tracery, and regretted that for us there was no "pale moonlight" in which to see it in still greater perfection. Still, we did *not* find that

> "the gay beams of lightsome day
> Gild, but to flout, the ruins gray."

We have made a deeply interesting visit to Abbotsford; driving through a pleasant, picturesque country, *all* of which seemed associated with the "great magician." On our way there, from Melrose, we made a little détour, and drove through the grounds of Chiefswood, where Mr. and Mrs. Lockhart once resided, and where Sir

Walter Scott so frequently took refuge, when he desired quiet. The prattling brook, and shady lane, by which the grounds are entered, recalled *him,* and his visits to the cheerful home of his beloved daughter, and we could imagine him seated on that porch, with his darling grand-child, John Hugh Lockhart at his knee. "Huntley Burn," too, where his friends, the Fergussons, used to welcome him, was near at hand, and we looked with deep interest upon the place where had once resided those whom he so tenderly loved. "A happier circle, (says Lockhart,) never met—but now those bright eyes are forever closed in dust—those gay voices forever silent."

We found Abbotsford lying low on the banks of the Tweed, and hidden from the road by trees. The house is a picturesque and curious structure, and the effect is very striking, although it is by no means so spacious as the pictures represent. The entrance hall is tastefully hung with armor, antlers, weapons, and many interesting relics—among them, the keys of the old Tolbooth prison in Edinburgh.

Then, in other rooms, there are pictures—some very rare and valuable—one of them, a head of Mary Queen of Scots, after her execution, is an original, and Sir Walter Scott would never suffer a copy to be taken. There is also a grotesque picture of Queen Elizabeth in fancy costume, which is anything but flattering. The family portraits interested us more than anything else, and we were shown several of the poet, taken at different times, those of his early boyhood looking wonderfully like those taken in his manhood.

There are portraits of Lady Scott and Mrs. Lockhart—a lovely picture of Miss Anne Scott, a bright-eyed brunette ; and a full length likeness of the last Sir Walter—a tall, handsome young man in uniform. There is also a curious portrait of Sir Walter's great grandfather, who allowed his full beard to grow after the execution of Charles I.

The library contains several thousand volumes, carefully protected by an iron grating. In this room is the bust of Scott by Chantrey, full of life and expression. There are also a number of ebony chairs presented to Sir Walter by George IV. The room adjoining was his private room, or study, with the chair remaining in the position in which he sat, and the desk at which he wrote. The walls of the room are lined with books, with a small gallery running around the whole, and a private staircase by which he came from his bed, or dressing-room, at pleasure. When he told the Duchess of St. Albans that he could come into his room by this private way, and work and write as much as he pleased "without any one's being the wiser for it," she replied, "that is impossible"—a compliment both graceful and true.

In a glass case are preserved the clothes Sir Walter last wore — the broad-skirted blue coat with large buttons, the trowsers of shepherd's plaid, the heavy shoes, the broad-brimmed white hat, and stout walking-stick, all looked so much as if they were to be worn again, and made his presence seem so recent, that one involuntarily spoke low, and glanced towards the door at which he used to enter.

The drawing-room is a lovely apartment, with a large bay window looking out upon the Tweed, and the hills opposite. Here, surrounded by his children, his great heart ceased to beat on the twenty-first of September, eighteen hundred and thirty-two. A short time before, he had asked to be wheeled about his rooms, and this was done for an hour or more, while he said again and again, "I have seen much, but nothing like my ain house." Then was read to him from the "one book" to which he desired to listen, "Let not your heart be troubled. In my Father's house are many mansions—I go to prepare a place for you." So with those sweet words of comfort in his ear, and "God bless you all," upon his lips, he breathed his last.

"It was a beautiful day," says Lockhart,—"so warm that every window was wide open, and so perfectly still, that the sound of all others most delicious to his ear, the gentle ripple of the Tweed over its pebbles, was distinctly audible, as we knelt around his bed, and his eldest son kissed, and closed his eyes."

As we stood, in silence, by that open window, with the Tweed still rippling over its pebbly bed, it seemed hardly possible that thirty-six years had passed away since that most touching scene occurred, on that very spot.

From Abbotsford, we drove to Dryburgh Abbey, the picturesque and ivy-grown ruin, where, in the burial-ground of his ancestors, the Haliburtons, Sir Walter is buried. It lies off the public road, in the midst of noble trees—among them some grand old yews—one of which is said to be of the same age as the Abbey, which dates back to eleven hundred and fifty. Columns, arches and windows still remain to show that the structure must once have been of great size and architectural beauty, while the ivy creeping all over the walls, and covering them with a thick matting of shining foliage, or hanging in graceful festoons, only makes the ruin still more beautiful. Beneath one of the arches of St. Mary's aisle, enclosed by an iron railing, lie the remains of Sir Walter Scott. A simple granite slab, raised two feet from the ground, with his name and the date of his death, is placed over his grave. On each side, are the tombs of his wife and son, the late Sir Walter, and at his feet lie the remains of John Gibson Lockhart. It is a calm, lovely spot—silent and solemn—and seems a fitting burial-place for one whose genius has given such life to all these memorials of departed centuries, and who, in the midst of his glory, suffered and sorrowed so deeply.

There is no bridge over the Tweed near the Abbey, and we were rowed over in a skiff, which is the only mode of crossing the river. The man told us that there had been nearly eleven thousand visitors to Dryburgh during the summer.

Edinburgh, September 22

Our stay of several days in this strangely picturesque and weird-looking town, has been somewhat marred by almost constant rain, or genuine Scotch mist, which has made all the distant views quite indistinct. Yet there have been times, when Arthur's Seat and the Salisbury Crags have stood out in all their beauty and grandeur, while the quaint old town itself is full of interest, even in a drizzling rain.

Certainly, never was there a more curious place than "Auld Reekie," with its old and new town, separated by a broad and deep ravine. The old city still has its narrow streets, intersected by *closes* and *wynds*, (that is, lanes and alleys,) and tumble down houses from six to ten stories high, in which the population is so immense, that the houses overflow into the streets and sidewalks, making it a matter of skill to get safely through the crowd, sometimes.

The new town wears a very different aspect; having wide streets, handsome shops, elegant mansions, fashionable hotels, public squares, monuments and statues. In front of our Hotel is the beautiful Gothic monument erected to the memory of Sir Walter Scott, which is two hundred feet high, and contains the noble statue of the poet by Chantrey, represented in a sitting posture, draped in a plaid, with his faithful dog at his feet; while in various niches are sculptured impersonations of the characters portrayed in his writings. One could not but think of the sonnet of one of our own poets, in looking upon the beautiful structure.

"'Tis said that 'mid the Alps and Pyrenees,
And other lofty mountains, and in groves,
And hidden places where the bandit roves,
Uptowering piles of stones the traveller sees
That mark the spot where some have fallen and died:
For them these shapless monuments are reared,
And, though to none who passes by endeared,
Each from his journeyings will turn aside
To cast his mite upon the rising moles,
And guard the memory of the lost unknown:
In this a deep, strong sentiment is shown—
A kindred for the dead in living souls.
If such, oh, world-renowned, *thy* grave could be,
An Alp would rise, a monument to thee!"

The royal castle on the brow of a precipice is a confused pile of buildings of different ages, and dates so far back that its origin is clouded in obscurity, but it is full of historical and romantic interest. The plain, sombre apartments in the most ancient part of the castle were occupied by Queen Mary; and in a small dressing-room, James VI., in whom the crowns of England and Scotland were united, was born. Over the door there is a curious inscription in black letter, commemorating the event, and invoking blessings on the child.

One shudders in looking out of the little window, upon the precipice beneath, where, when only eight days old, the future monarch was let down in a basket, to be conveyed to a place of greater safety, by friends who were waiting at the foot of the rocks. We looked at the regalia with great interest, from the fact that the crown, sceptre, and sword of state, were for a long time hidden in an old oak chest, and that they were connected with great historical events for years. In themselves, they are of comparatively little value.

From the ramparts of the castle, we had a superb view of the town and its surroundings, and saw the gigantic piece of artillery, called Mons Meg—a cannon cast in the early part of fifteen hundred, and named after the man who cast it, and his wife, Meg. In sixteen hundred and eighty-two, it burst, when firing a salute for the Duke of York, and has not been used since.

Holyrood Palace, although neither grand nor

beautiful in itself, has so many historical and deeply tragic associations connected with it, that it is impossible not to feel awed when within its walls. We made a hasty visit to the picture gallery, which contains portraits of royal and eminent Scotch personages, but the paintings are extremely poor, and not considered genuine. Then we entered the apartments of the unfortunate Queen, which are preserved as they were when occupied by her, with the very same tapestry, hangings, and much of the same furniture. The bed, with its velvet canopy, tattered and time-worn, with a piece of one of the blankets, about a foot square upon it, stands as it did when her lovely limbs reposed upon it. The mirror too, which had so often given back the reflection of her beautiful face, hangs upon the wall, and her work-table, and some articles of her toilette are still there. The little room in which the queen sat at supper with David Rizzio, on the night of his murder, adjoins the sleeping apartment, and a private staircase leads to it, from the chapel below, up which the assassins came and made those fifty-six wounds, which forever stained the floor of the ante-chamber where Rizzio lay all night. In the little supper-room, is a glass altar-piece, a painting of the Virgin Mary, which has a huge crack in the centre, said to have been made by the fist of John Knox, when remonstrating very earnestly with the Queen on the error of her ways.

The ruins of the chapel of Holyrood Abbey, show that it must have been a magnificent edifice ; but it has a dreary look now, and is only used as a burial-place for illustrious persons—some of the former kings of Scotland having been buried there. In the roofless choir, the altar stood, before which the beautiful Mary and Lord Darnley were united in an unfortunate marriage.

We greatly enjoyed a drive to Calton Hill one day, from which we had charming views of the entire town, country, frith and sea. There is an observatory on its summit, and monuments to Nelson, Playfair and Dugald Stewart. Near it are seen the monuments of Hume and Burns. Afterwards we drove through the curious streets to the quaint old house of John Knox, and to the house in Castle Street where Sir Walter Scott lived several years before he built Abbotsford. In the Greyfriars churchyard we found many very interesting monuments, and some odd epitaphs in memory of the Covenanters.

Edinburgh abounds in charitable institutions, and we visited with pleasure, the "Trades Maiden Hospital," where the daughters of worthy trades-people are educated and cared for. We found it delightfully situated in the midst of pretty grounds, with a matron whose sweet voice and charming Scotch accent were quite fascinating. Everything seemed to be sensibly, kindly and pleasantly arranged for the inmates, who are here thoroughly prepared to fill various positions in life.

We have had the pleasure of hearing the Rev. Horatius Bonar preach. The sermon was rather fragmentary, but a clear presentation of the doctrine of the personality, divinity and offices of the Holy Spirit. His manner is very peculiar, at first slow and drawling, and afterwards quite animated. He rests his body upon the cushion of the pulpit, and very seldom stands upright. It was pleasant to look upon the author of those beautiful "Hymns of Faith and Hope," and afterwards to meet him at his own hospitable board, where we also met the mother of the sainted Mary Lundie Duncan.

The churches are well filled here, and the congregations most attentive; young and old, Bible in Land, always turning to the texts quoted by the preacher during his sermon. All join in the singing, and if the music is not artistic, it is at least more like worship, than if performed by a hired quartette. On Sunday evening we heard some street preaching which gathered a large and well-behaved crowd, many of whom remained standing a long time to listen.

Stirling.

On our way to this town, so delightfully situated on the River Forth, we passed Linlithgow Palace, an ancient ruin placed upon an eminence near the lake where Mary Queen of Scots was born on the seventh of December, fifteen hundred and forty-two.

Stirling Castle is grandly situated on the brow of a precipitous rock. The view from the walls is most extensive and magnificent, comprising the highland mountains Ben Lomond, Ben Ledi, and numerous other *Bens*, in one direction ; while nearer, is a richly cultivated country, with the rivers Forth, Frith and Allan forming the most beautiful curves, and visible for miles, winding among woods and hills. On one of these latter is a fine monument to Sir William Wallace, two hundred and fifty feet high. The once bloody battle-fields of Falkirk, Cambuskenneth and Bannockburn are in full view, and the castle of Edinburgh is seen on the horizon, far away. To add to our enjoyment, the noble Forty-second regiment, which gained such renown in the Crimea, came out to drill soon after we entered the castle grounds, and the bagpipes, warlike music, and wonderful evolutions of these splendid-looking men in their Highland costume, made the whole scene most enchanting.

We were much favored in being escorted about the castle by a soldier belonging to the Forty-second regiment, who, although a young man, had been ten years in India, and two or three in the Crimea. He wore many badges, showing in what battles he had fought, but that which had the highest value in his estimation, was the one which the government had given him for bravery. While walking about, we saw several soldiers undergoing punishment for desertion. The punishment consisted in picking up and carrying cannon-balls from one point to another, about ten feet. They had done this for an hour at a time, at brief intervals, for many days. We quite agreed with our pleasant guide, that it was a senseless kind of punishment, and it would be much better to make them do something useful.

Mary Queen of Scots was crowned at Stirling, and James VI. was educated here. Indeed, the castle is connected with the history of Scotland for many centuries. We were shown the tower room where James II. assassinated William, Earl of Douglas, on account of his defiance of his authority.

> "The tower within whose circuit dread
> A Douglas, by his sovereign bled."

An incident occurred while we were in this room, which amused us very much. Among the visitors was a well-dressed gentleman, whom the woman who has charge of the room took to be Lord Napier of Magdala, for some reason or other. So the good old soul was wonderfully elated by the idea that she was receiving the hero of Abyssinia. In the mean time, the gentleman walked about with his wife, in the most unpretending manner possible, while the woman's face beamed with smiles, courtesying to the very ground whenever she was addressed, and continually using the words "my lady" and "your ladyship," when addressed by the lady. She also informed them that she had had the honor of receiving the Queen, and the Prince of Wales. Of course, our own humble party were quite thrown in the shade, and for a few moments we all thought we were in the presence of the great warrior. We were soon undeceived, however, and left the place wondering how the beaming woman would feel when she heard that she had dispensed all those fascinating smiles upon plain Mr. S——, of London!

On leaving the castle we visited the old Greyfriars churchyard, where are monuments to some of the Reformers, and a beautiful group in marble under a glass case, of the Virgin Martyr of the ocean wave, Margaret Wilson of Glenvarnock, and her sister Agnes, who preferred drowning, to renouncing their faith. An angel stands over them in a protecting attitude, while the faces of the young martyrs, are most saint-like in expression, and full of holy faith.

Glasgow.

Our journey here has been delightful, and we feel that too much praise cannot be bestowed upon the weather, which is generally not agreeable at this season. Clear bright sunshine has been our portion, and we have greatly enjoyed our elevation on the top of a stage coach many miles of our way. From Callender we came to the castellated Hotel in the Trossachs, with the unpronounceable name of Ardcheanachrochan, which means "the eminence at the end of the knoll."

Loch Achray lies in quiet beauty in front of the house, and at the back is Ben Aan with its magnificent peak of bare rock. The drive all the way from Callender, was full of interest and beauty, and Roderick Dhu and James Fitz-James seemed real characters to us, as we followed their footsteps. We spent the night in this enchanting spot, and were put to sleep by the humming noise of a bagpipe beneath our window, which sounded much like a huge mosquito. If it be true, as Sir Walter Scott has said, that "Highlanders reach the highest point of happiness when twenty-four bagpipe players are assembled together in a small room, all playing at the same time different tunes," we were thankful to have been spared such a musical treat. We found one quite sufficient.

The next morning we drove through the magnificent defile of the Trossachs to Loch Katrine, which burst upon us in exquisite loveliness—"fair Ellen's" isle,

> "Where for retreat in dangerous hour
> Some chief had framed a rustic bower,"

being in full view. We took a pleasant little steamer at the lake, and soon found ourselves gazing upon island, shore, and mountains "that like giants stand—" a combination of sylvan beauty and alpine grandeur. Loch Katrine is of a serpentine form, encircled by lofty mountains, and is ten miles in length. The immense quantities of fern upon the hills, in the yellow and brown coloring of autumn, gave a very peculiar effect, while the lake itself, as we looked upon it from the deck of the steamboat, appeared almost black, so dark is the color of the water. We seemed to be, indeed, in the midst of an enchanted land; and the hour spent upon that lovely lake was one of pure and perfect delight.

> "So wondrous wild, the whole might seem
> The scenery of a fairy dream."

At Stronachlachar Pier, near the west end of the lake, we were met by two coaches, prepared to convey passengers over the Highlands, and a scrambling for seats commenced which was both annoying and amusing. As we could only ascend to the top of the coach by means of a long ladder, the one who by dint of pushing others back, succeeded in mounting first, of course secured a seat. There being room enough for all, however, no necessity existed for such a rudeness, and we were quite surprised to see it, and glad that our own countrymen were not the uncourteous ones on this occasion. At length we were all comfortably seated on the dizzy height, and drove five miles over a rugged road with glorious views all the way, to Inversnaid.

In a lonely spot, not far from the road, Rob Roy once resided, and near at hand is the hut where it is said his wife, Helen MacGregor, first saw the light. We also passed the ruins of Inversnaid Fort, which was erected by government in seventeen hundred and thirteen, to check the MacGregors, and which was at one time the quarters of General Wolfe, of Quebec memory. We remained long enough at Inversnaid to wander about the pretty little rivulet and cascade, which Wordsworth has immortalized in his "Highland Girl," and then took the steamer on Loch Lomond, "the lake full of islands." This is called "the pride of Scottish Lakes," and filled as it is with beautiful islands, of every form and outline, lofty mountains stretching away in the distance at the *north*, grand Ben Lomond towering above them all; and at the *south,* all fertility and loveliness—it is, indeed, gloriously beautiful and sublime.

There are many charming villas in full view, some of them situated on promontories, which jut out into the lake. Among them, is Rossdow, the splendid residence of Sir James Colquhoun; a lovely spot.

At Balloch, we took the cars for Glasgow, passing the grand old Castle of Dumbarton, securely seated upon a rocky eminence.

We are now at a pleasant hotel on George's Square, which is spacious and prettily laid out, with a noble column in it, surmounted by a statue of Sir Walter Scott robed in a shepherd's plaid. There are also fine monuments to Sir John Moore and James Watts, standing in the square.

Glasgow, for a manufacturing town, is quite handsome, and we have been much interested in the immense amount of shipping to be seen here at the mouth of the Clyde. They are also enlarging and beautifying the town very much, and it exhibits present thrift and prosperity, very strikingly.

Kelvin Grove park is a charming spot, with many elegant residences overlooking it, and is a great place of resort; "Let us haste to Kelvin Grove, bonnie lassie, O," being evidently sung with good effect, to the fair maidens of Glasgow.

The Cathedral is a striking relic of antiquity, commandingly situated, with a massive grandeur about it, but it is rather gloomy than otherwise. The crypts beneath are very extensive and graceful, and were intended as a place of interment for the dignitaries of the Cathedral.

An old churchyard called the Necropolis, rises in terraces back of the Cathedral, and in it are some very beautiful monuments, among which, one erected to the memory of John Knox is most conspicuous. The cemetery, with its flowers, shrubbery, trees and gravel walks, looks more like a pleasure-ground, than a resting-place for the dead.

We have been struck here, as we were in Edinburgh, with the number of barefooted and ragged women, whom we meet in the streets. None but *very* well-dressed women seem to wear shoes and stockings at all, although the weather is now decidedly chilly.

Glasgow abounds in religious, charitable, and philanthropic institutions, and we were much interested in the "Night Asylum for the Houseless," which was instituted thirty years ago for the benefit of the miserable beings who are without friends or shelter. All are admitted who apply, supper is provided for all, and breakfast for the women and children, as well as for such of the men as appear to be most in want. Often the applicants are quite respectable, but out of employment from no fault of their own, and this house affords them a temporary shelter. That it is *needed*, is shown from the fact that during the past year thirty-six thousand three hundred and forty-nine persons have been received and cared for. Some of the lodgings are not very luxurious, as they consist of a wooden pillow upon a hard floor, with a coarse mat to wrap around the sleeper. The floor is divided into compartments, by a low board, which denotes the space each one is to occupy, and several men share the same room, which is thoroughly scrubbed every day. The women are rather better cared for, and everything is very neat and well arranged. They generally have more applications on Saturday nights than at other times, and there is a spacious chapel connected with the institution, in which they all assemble on Sunday morning, for service.

Ayr, September 28.

We are again at one of the "pilgrim shrines" which it is impossible to visit without deep emotion.

We find Ayr a pleasant flourishing town, with its "twa brigs," immortalized by Burns, still standing, one of which was said to have been built in the twelfth century, and is a quaint-looking structure. There is little in the town associated with Burns, so we drove at once to Alloway, where stands the "clay bigging" with its thatched roof, in which the poet was born. There are only two apartments in the house, both on the ground floor—one a kitchen, and the other a sitting-room. Both have very small windows, and very low ceilings. The kitchen has a recess for a bed, and here Robert Burns first opened his eyes upon a world which gave him little pleasure, but which remembers him *now*, with sympathy and tenderness. Near the cottage stands "Alloway's auld haunted kirk," with the walls well preserved, and no roof—a picturesque edifice, from one of the windows of which Tam O'Shanter peeped at the witches. The wood-work has all been taken away to form snuff-boxes, and other memorials, and it has also been necessary to replace the tombstone of Burns' father—the old one having been carried off in fragments.

From the kirk we went to the monument, which stands on a bank of the river Doon, and is of fine white freestone. In a circular apartment, on the ground floor, are some relics of the poet—a most touching one being the Bible in two volumes, which Burns gave to his Highland Mary at their betrothal; with his name, and masons' mark, in both volumes. The original copy of the familiar song, "Scots wha hae wi Wallace bled," in the hand-writing of the poet, with his interlineations and corrections, hangs upon the wall, in a frame. A song, of which he modestly writes, when enclosing it to a friend—"I think it has some merit."

On leaving the monument, we sat and strolled on the lovely banks of Bonnie Doon—stood upon the "auld brig"—quoted snatches of songs and poems, and everything seemed to belong to Burns, and to be a part of his life and spirit. It was a great delight to appropriate the lines of Halleck—

> "I've stood beside the cottage bed,
> Where the bard-peasant first drew breath ;

A straw-thatched roof above his head,
  A straw-wrought couch beneath.

And I have stood beside the pile,
  His monument—that tells to Heaven
The homage of earth's proudest isle,
  To that bard-peasant given!"

Windermere.

The queen of the English lakes lies in graceful beauty in full view from our hotel, and while it can hardly challenge admiration on the score of grandeur, it is a charming picture of quiet loveliness, upon which we are never weary of gazing. Although the largest of the cluster of lakes, it is only eleven miles in length, and one in breadth. Its margin is occupied by gentle eminences, which are cultivated wherever the trees have been cleared away, and villas and cottages gleaming amid the woods are visible in every direction, giving a cheerful character to the scene. It is not strange that poets should have sought this spot, and revelled in its beauties.

Near our hotel, are the grounds of Professor Wilson, who spent much of his palmiest time here, and those must indeed have been glorious days, when Sir Walter Scott, Canning, Lockhart, Wordsworth, Southey and Coleridge met here, to enjoy with him "brilliant cavalcades through the woods in the mornings, and delicious boatings on the lake by moonlight."

We have taken a charming drive to Keswick, passing Rydal, Grasmere, Thirlmere and Derwentwater lakes, with their surroundings of mountains, fir-crested rocks, and fertile valleys. The whole way seemed classic ground, so associated is that entire region with the bright spirits who have dwelt there.

We visited Fox Howe, the favorite home of the noble Dr. Arnold, where he, every year, sought recreation and repose, from the cares of Rugby: the knoll where Harriet Martineau is resting after a busy and useful life, in an ivy-covered cottage, with a pretty lawn, and glorious views: Doves Nest, where Mrs. Hemans found peace and happiness for a time; thus writing to a friend—"I am so delighted with this spot that I scarcely know how I shall leave it. The situation is one of the deepest retirement; but the bright lake before me, with all its fairy barks and sails, glancing like 'things of life' over its blue waters, prevents the solitude from being overshadowed by anything like sadness."

Knab Cottage, where De Quincy once lived,

and Hartley Coleridge died, is charmingly situated near Rydal Lake, although so near the road, that there is but little shrubbery in front of it, in which it differs from most of the cottages in this neighborhood. Rydal Mount is now unoccupied, but we stood in the porch with the word "salve," upon its mosaic pavement, and thought of the noble poet of nature, who had so often stood there to welcome his guests, but who had been carried thence, never to return. From the little lawn in front of the cottage, we looked upon the view in which he delighted: Rydal Water at the foot of the hill, Windermere, the valley of the Rothay, and rugged Loughrigg. Then we walked upon the two little terraces, the favorite composing ground of the poet, and sat upon his favorite rustic seat, thinking of the charm he had given to all this scenery by his writings, and of his pure, loving nature. In the corner of Grasmere churchyard, we found his last resting-place, with the stream within hearing, whose song was so dear to him in life. He is surrounded by his family, and poor Hartley Coleridge lies near.

Nothing could be more simple than the headstones at the graves of the Wordsworth family, and we were greatly touched by an inscription on a little stone, near that of the poet :

> "Here lieth the body of Thomas, the son of William and Mary Wordsworth. He died on the 1st of December, 1812.
>
> "Six months to six years added, he remained
> Upon this sinful earth, by sin unstained.
> O, blessed Lord, whose mercy then removed
> A child whom every eye that looked on loved,
> Support us, teach us calmly to resign
> What we possessed, and now is wholly thine."

We found Keswick a manufacturing town with a magnificent array of mountains about it, and cheerful, pleasant streets. Linsey-woolsey stuffs, edge-tools and pencils are made here, and the odor of cedar attracted us to the manufactory of the latter, where we saw the process of making them.

Greta Hall stands on an eminence directly opposite the factory, and it was difficult to fix one's mind on cedar and plumbago, with the home of Southey so near. It is charmingly situated on the banks of the river Greta, surrounded by scenery which combines both beauty and grandeur, and here the poet-laureate passed many "golden days" in his happy home circle, with views from his windows which were of themselves a recreation to his mind, and a feast to the eye. How bright and cheerful he once made that home, his letters plainly show, and it is sad to think of the shadow which at last fell upon that "boy's heart," which, as he wrote to a friend, "is as great a blessing in carrying one through the world, as to have a child's spirit will be in fitting us for the next."

In the Crosthwaite church, we saw the beautiful recumbent statue of Southey, and in the pleasant churchyard, with grand old Skiddaw in full view, his quiet grave. Near him, sleeps his beloved Edith, and the darling boy of ten, whose endearing qualities, singularly beautiful and gentle disposition, and wonderful aptitude for study, were such a source of heartfelt delight to his fond father—so much so, that on the day of his death, he says, in a letter communicating the sad intelligence, "You are far from knowing how large a portion of my hopes and happiness will be laid in the grave with Herbert. For years it has been my daily prayer that I might be spared this affliction." Yet, long before, he had shown on whom he relied, in a letter to the same friend: "I have a deep conviction that whatever affliction I have ever endured, or yet have to endure, is dispensed to me in mercy and in love." The old sexton, as he took us to this peaceful resting-place, in that quiet churchyard, delighted in telling us of Southey's goodness, and of the noble little boy whom he remembered so well.

Liverpool, Oct. 8.

After an absence of five months, we find ourselves again beneath the pleasant roof which sheltered us when we had just commenced our wanderings. Now, with grateful hearts, we accept the same kind shelter, feeling how tenderly we have been cared for, both on the sea and on the land. Our stay here has been diversified by a charming visit to Chester, the quaint old town, which was a Roman military station in the days of Julius Cæsar. The wall which entirely surrounds the city, and is broad enough for a promenade, has been standing nearly a thousand years, and from it delightful views may be obtained in all directions.

The houses are so quaint and peculiar, that one can hardly believe the town is really in England. The sidewalks are formed by the basements of the houses, and are roofed by their second stories. The covered ways, thus formed, are lined with shops of every description, and above are the dwelling-houses. In many instances, the upper story projects over the next lower, so that the occupants of the fourth floor, on opposite sides of the street, are brought very near together. Then there are narrow lanes and alleys—queer, antique houses, with small diamond-shaped panes in the sashes. Every house, nearly, looking as if it had a history, and had stood for centuries.

The Cathedral is a venerable structure, with crumbling walls, and huge ancient trees, growing where some of the cloisters of the adjacent abbey stood. It contains many ancient monuments, rudely sculptured ; mosaic altar-pieces, painted glass, and is altogether a most curious and interesting specimen of past ages.

From Chester, we went to the lovely Vale of Llangollen, stopping long enough at Ruabon to walk to Wynnstay Park, the beautiful residence of Sir Watkin Williams Wynn, with a noble avenue of elms, three quarters of a mile long, leading to the house. The Vale of Llangollen, with the river Dee flowing through it, has long been celebrated for its beauty, and as we walked from the cars to the Hand Hotel, we felt that this must be, indeed, "the sweetest and quietest spot on earth"—one in which our willing souls would gladly stay for weeks, not days. But that was impossible ; so, during our brief sojourn we drank in all that we could, and remember with great delight our hurried visit to this charming vale. The beautiful and picturesque remains of Vale Crucis Abbey, which was founded in twelve hundred, interested us very much. They are covered with ivy, and shaded with lofty ash trees, and there are some grim forms of knights sculptured in gray stone, lying upon the floor, which have been there for centuries, and are very curious. It was evidently a large and imposing structure at one time, and is lovely in its decay.

We drove to Plas Newydd the pretty little cottage, with antique sculptures over the door, where the ladies of Llangollen, Lady Eleanor Butler and Miss Sarah Ponsonby, two women of wealth and high station, devoted their lives to each other for nearly threescore years ; and for a quarter of a century, never spent twenty-four hours at a time out of their happy valley. The situation of the house is very fine, and in the days of those elegant and cultivated ladies, the place must have been beautiful. Here, too, they were sought by the first characters of the age, both as to rank and talents, whom they entertained with generous hospitality, while declaring that neither the long summer's day, nor winter's night, ever inspired a wish to return to the world they had forsaken. A faithful servant lived with them thirty years, and now, beneath a triangular tomb, in the shadow of the old church, with the river Dee running merrily by, the ladies and their devoted friend rest together, side by side. The two friends were only separated by death a little more than two years; Lady Eleanor Butler dying on the second of June, eighteen hundred and twenty-nine, aged ninety years, and Sarah Ponsonby, December ninth, eighteen hundred and thirty-one, aged seventy-six. Mary Carryl died in eighteen hundred and nine, and the inscription to her memory ends with the lines

> "Reared by two friends, who will her loss bemoan,
> Till with her ashes, here shall rest their own."

On Saturday, the tenth of October, we embarked at Liverpool, on the noble steamship Russia again, for our homeward voyage. We reached Queenstown early on the morning of the eleventh, and remained there several hours. It was a lovely day, and the harbor and surrounding country appeared very attractive. The confusion was so great that all religious service was omitted. This surprised us, as the English habit is very fixed in such matters.

Irish women made their appearance on deck, with apples, laces, and bog-wood ornaments to sell, and drove a brisk trade. It reminded us of what we had so often seen on the continent, but were not quite prepared to see in Great Britain.

Our passage home was enlivened by hard winds and an uneasy sea most of the way, but our splendid steamer weathered every gale, and on Wednesday, October twenty-first, we landed in New York. As we drove up Fifth Avenue, after a journey of just six months, which we shall always remember with the deepest gratitude, one of our party exclaimed enthusiastically, "We have not seen so beautiful a street as this, *anywhere!*" To which there was no dissenting voice, and we all felt glad and proud to say,

"This is my own—my native land."

www.ingramcontent.com/pod-product-compliance
Lightning Source LLC
LaVergne TN
LVHW010214110826
845151LV00004B/1084

9781425528195